Small Hours

Winner of the 2014 T. S. Eliot Prize

The T. S. Eliot Prize for Poetry is an annual award sponsored by Truman State University Press for the best unpublished book-length collection of poetry in English, in honor of native Missourian T. S. Eliot's considerable intellectual and artistic legacy.

Judge for 2014: Dorianne Laux

Small Hours

Ilyse Kusnetz

New Odyssey Series
Truman State University Press
Kirksville, Missouri

Copyright © 2014 Truman State University Press, Kirksville, Missouri, 63501
All rights reserved
tsup.truman.edu

Cover art: Remedios Varo, *Papilla estelar*, 1958 © 2014 Artists Rights Society
(ARS), New York / VEGAP, Madrid

Cover design: Teresa Wheeler

Library of Congress Cataloging-in-Publication Data
Kusnetz, Ilyse, 1966–
[Poems. Selections]
Small hours / Ilyse Kusnetz.
        pages cm — (New odyssey series)
ISBN 978-1-61248-128-9 (alk. paper) — ISBN 978-1-61248-129-6 (e-book)
I. Title.
PS3611.U7395A6 2014
811'.6—dc23

                                                    2014016930

The paper in this publication meets or exceeds the minimum requirements of
the American National Standard for Information Sciences—Permanence of
Paper for Printed Library Materials, ANSI Z39.48–1992.

for Brian

Contents

Acknowledgments

I would like to thank the following individuals:

Tony Barnstone, Stacey Lynn Brown, Kim Buchheit, Susan Dauer, Charlotte Davidson, Stephen Dunn, Carolyn Forché, Kelle Groom, Lee Herrick, Jane Hirshfield, Ilya Kaminsky, Kathy Kincer, Krista Knopper, Dorianne Laux, Thomas Lynch, Michele McArdle, Laura McCullough, Joe Millar, Matt O'Donnell, Sharon Olds, April Ossmann, Nancy Rediger, Suzanne Roberts, Barbara Smith-Mandell and all the wonderful people at Truman State University Press, Melanie Stammbach, Cheryl Stiles, Dan Veach, the Valencia Foundation, and Sholeh Wolpe.

Thanks also to my friends and colleagues whose support was invaluable, and to the members of the Movie Club who took such good care of me.

A special thanks goes to my family for their belief in me all these years, and most of all, I would like to thank my husband, Brian Turner. I could not have written this book without his unconditional love and encouragement, and his unerring poetic eye.

Grateful acknowledgment is made to the editors and publishers of the following publications in which some of these poems first appeared.

"*Ideal City*, Dream Sequence" and "Galileo's Finger" appeared in *Artful Dodge*.

"A Hampshire Field at Sunset" appeared in *Atlanta Review*.

"Buddha's Garden" appeared in *Barely South Review*.

"L'Annunziazione" appeared in the *Cimarron Review*.

"Perseids, New Smyrna Beach" appeared in the *Cincinnati Review*.

"Archival Footage," "Gift Horse," "Letter to Scientists," "My Uncle as Erwin Schrödinger," and "The Sultan's Dwarves" appeared in *Connotation Press: An Online Artifact*.

"My Father in the Coast Guard, 1946" appeared in *Crab Orchard Review*.

"Before I Am Downloaded into a Most Excellent Robot Body" appeared in *Devouring the Green: Fear of a Transhuman Planet*.

"Magpie," "My Father in the Coast Guard, 1946," "Gift Horse," "Archival Footage," "Match Girls," "A Hampshire Field at Sunset," "L'Annunziazione," and "*Ideal City*, Dream Sequence" appear at http://www.fishousepoems.org/?s=ilyse+kusnetz.

"Marie Antoinette's Beech Tree" and an earlier version of "Bleach" appeared in *ISLE: Interdisciplinary Studies in Literature and Environment*.

"Magpie" appeared in *Kestrel*.

"Classified" appeared in *MiPOesias*.

"The Birth of Godzilla" appeared in the anthology *Monstrous Verse: Angels, Demons, Vampires, Ghosts, and Fabulous Beasts*.

"Invisible Children" appeared in *Poet Lore*.

"Match Girls" appeared in *Rattle*, and was reprinted in *Women's Voices for Change* (http://womensvoicesforchange.org) and *The Best of Kore Press, 2012: Poetry*.

"The Eagle's Nest" appeared in *Stone Canoe*.

"Grin" appeared in *The Best of Kore Press, 2012: Poetry*.

"Blue Amber" appeared in *The Book of Scented Things*.

"Kilter" and "Torture" appeared in *The Chariton Review*.

"Röntgen's Wife" appeared in *Women's Voices for Change* (http://womensvoicesforchange.org).

1

Match Girls

In the factories of America
during the nineteenth century, girls

hired to make matches
would dip the match ends

into a chemical vat, then
lick the tips to make them stiff.

Phosphorous vapor
filled the air, a poison

about which no one warned them,
so when their teeth fell out,

and their jaws rotted
like bad fruit, it was too late.

It was not the first time
such things happened.

Bent at their workstations,
women in the eighteenth century

cured ladies' hats with mercury.
Their legacy—blushing, aching limbs,

a plague of rashes, parchment-thin
pages of sloughed skin, curled

and cracked, minds deranged.
They could not know they shared a fate

with Emperor Qin Shi Huang, who
seeking eternal life, swallowed pills

laced with mercury. He built the Great Wall
and unified China, then outlawed all religions

not sanctioned by the state,
burned treatises on history, politics, and art.

Scholars who dared possess such things,
he buried alive. His body lies

in a vast mausoleum, guarded
by a terracotta army.

Of the factory girls, mouths opening
below earth, their bodies

burning like forbidden books,
we know almost nothing.

Magpie

Never mind how they met. Sometimes in stories,
the inexplicable happens. At first, the river of the universe
is too wide for the parted lovers to cross.
Their tears call the birds from the sky, and flocks of magpies gather
to form a bridge, wingtip to wingtip, offering up their hollow
bones for love's sake, which is why the magpie is considered
a sacred bird, and if at dawn you spy only one, you must say
Good morning, Mr. Magpie. Where is your wife today? And this
is because of Orihime, the Weaving Princess, daughter of Tentei
the Sky King, and Hikoboshi the Cow Herder, who wait on the
        glittering
banks of Amanogawa, the infinite, longing river we must cross
or be lost, drowned in the night's water, one feather dancing upon
        another.

Invisible Children

People can get used to anything.
Each day cars would wait patiently
as crossing guards ushered
rows of invisible schoolchildren to safety.

Teachers, ears sharpened like pencils, learned
to pinpoint each child's location and identity
by tracking the intricate Doppler of their voices,
divining the subtle shift of chairs.

Birds of laughter, shouts
zoomed across the playground—
the lone signs of the daring, a jingling
buck of swings, sneaker prints planted in the sand.

The candy shop proprietor, a practical man
resigned himself to chocolate bars
unwrapping themselves, gauzy bubbles
of gum expanding in mid-air.

Everyone played Marco Polo.
On birthdays and holidays, parents
layered *papier-mâché* over their
children's faces, sculpted impressions.

But often at night, a mother or father woke
to pace the silent corridors and rooms,
imagining here, the heated curve of a cheek,
there, like gentle bellows, the rib cage's rise and fall.

The War Years

Years my father paid a nickel for all-day movie Saturday at the
    People's Cinema,
could hop a train from Brooklyn to Manhattan, bebop at the
    Royal Roost,

big band at the Paramount—Gene Krupa drumming like a demon,
Harry James on the horn, loving that wicked brass like it was
    Betty Grable

before he got busted for coke and she left him. Years my father
rounded the corner of Saratoga Avenue and Livonia on the way
    to synagogue,

or past his grandfather hovering on the stoop, cigarette a seesaw
bobbing at the old man's lips. Years my father snuck into the
    Metropolitan,

memorizing the curves of *Reclining Odalisque*, how light fell
on Rembrandt's *Bathsheba*, the way pharaohs in sarcophagi

reminded him of his tante's old *matryoshkas*. Some afternoons,
    those years,
my father would stow his books and just wander—

his father, an arcade-owner, dead of a heart attack a week after
    LaGuardia
smashed the boroughs' pinball machines, while Uncle Lou planned
    union strikes,

asking, *Don't you think workers should have rights?* My father popped
carnie balloons for cash, played keno under the IRT, dreaming egg creams,

Coney Island hot dogs, the Dodgers at Ebbets Field. And though the war
was everywhere, it wasn't yet in the subtitled Soviet films

on the People's screen, or in elevated train cars, in bebop and big band,
in hushed and glowing galleries of brushstrokes and gilded graves

within graves, it wasn't in the jangling recoil of ball after ball, as if that boy
could simply fold up entire years and slip them in his pocket,

walk off into the future crooning *Sleepy Lagoon, We're deep in a spell*, and
I'll Get By, As long as I have you, as long as I have you.

Feeder

When we hang the bird feeder
from an oak tree in the yard,

first cardinals, then mockingbirds arrive,
then blue jays beaking at fallen

seeds in the grass, flitting into the boughs
to preen their white breasts.

In the dart and shiver of wings, a still
vibrating emptiness, the sudden

bend and flash of leaves,
we feel our own heart beating

the way, briefly, with gem-bright yearning
a wild thing comes to rest.

Chopping an Onion in the Kitchen, I Think of My Parents

What, after all, is left to say? The truth's worn thin
as an old sheet. Sometimes I imagine propping them up
against the place in memory they've stumbled, half-
asleep. I might in passing smooth her hair, or
comb it straight, or notch his wide tie further down
his neck, folding their hands gently, at last
very gently, lifting away her shadowy sadness,
tamping back the anger eager to char his mouth.
And here they can be young again, untouched
by grief or regret, the selves they once inhabited
like palimpsests, overwritten by the scratching pens
of the living, who cast their lives and say again:
they did the best they could, loved as they
knew how. Say it, now. That's all there is.

Röntgen's Wife

Each night the sun would ratchet down, he'd burnish
the X-ray plates with vinegar until they shone,

then seek her out, supper warming on the stove,
her soft touch on his arm. She remembered

the night he coaxed her into the lab, spread her fingers
gently in front of the glass, and counted off the seconds—

how the first X-ray ever created was proof of his love:
Portrait of a hand with wedding ring, diamond and band

like Saturn perched on her finger, each joint a moon,
glowing in the flesh's ghostly firmament.

I can see right through you, he'd joke, for the rest
of their lives. And she'd think how thin

her bones looked, curved like talons,
as if what lay concealed beneath a coat of skin,

unseen until he'd captured her, was flight.

My Father in the Coast Guard, 1946

New at sea,
laboring with
block and tackle,

he and his crew are
loading ammunition
onto the *Tampa*,

a 240-foot cutter,
when the sheave
breaks, and crates

of 3-inch .50-caliber
bullets begin
to plummet toward

the men below.
All let go of the rope
except my father.

He holds to that line
as he'd later hold
to all of us—

my mother, my brothers,
my sister and me,
until the skin peels

from his palms,
and the rope
slices through to bone.

Shrapnel

Here, a stagnant, nervous peace—
wood pigeons startling from crepe myrtles,

a lawn mower's muffled buzz,
dead horses of bicycles in driveways.

Drunk on Jack, our neighbors argue
a familiar, unsolvable equation—

transmuted by the kindness of walls,
their voices echo down the block

a call to prayer, but tonight
the gods of suburbia are busy elsewhere.

Perhaps they are watching over our children
whose nature it is, when left alone too long

with their unbearable heaviness, to flail
against what injures them, to make of themselves

a kind of weapon. Why are we surprised
when teenagers tie firecrackers to a stray dog's tail,

or strap rifles over their thin-boy shoulders
like messenger bags?

I think of Shrapnel setting targets in the field,
how each day he'd plan and test the limits

of his campaign, searching for a better way to inflict
damage, to expand the known radius of pain.

White Herons

My father's favorite joke went like this: The Lone Ranger
says to Tonto, *Why are the natives so angry?*

and Tonto replies, *Kemo Sabe, they are angry
from a previous movie.*

Perhaps he understood my mother, after all.
On the stereo, Sonny Boy Williamson

wailing *Help me, if you won't help me* his voice echoing
in the chorus of tree frogs at the lake where we walk,

cypress knees gathered like tiny, hooded monks,
Spanish moss bearding the oaks, white herons

in the papyrus, moonlight daubed on their
crested heads, shadows curving in the water,

still as birds in a Japanese woodblock print,
as the song of everything slakes our throats

and fills our lungs, the wings we hold inside ourselves,
white herons rising into the dark.

Small Hours

I was shocked that last Thanksgiving to see
my mother—life-long enemy of stray threads,
smudged faces, raised voices—in pajamas
at the dining room table, not wearing her wig,
hair a scatter of pin feathers
stuck to her scalp.

It was the last night she spent at home,
my father refusing to admit her decline
and so when he urged her *farther,*
a little farther, she collapsed
onto the bathroom floor. Still
he wouldn't dial the ambulance.

I remember her long-ago advice to me:
It takes fewer muscles to smile
than it does to frown,
as if unhappiness were only a facial expression,
the heart's desire wafting
along a flower-lined path of least resistance.

Weeks later, I stood beside her hospital bed.
Waking, she'd suck orange slices, clown smiles,
tongue so parched, each word she tried to utter
stuck in her mouth like driftwood,
though once during the small hours
I heard her sigh to herself, *Oh, well.*

Kilter

I'm nine years old, surprised
to hear my father, a working man,
a tinker of all things
mechanical, say *shim*.
On his lips
it seems a frivolous word, until he explains
It's a thing you slide underneath other things.
And this was to keep them
on an even kilter, to solve, like an equation,
the tick-tock of unsteadiness.
He shims a folded paper into place. *Not to be
confused with shivs*, he says,
which are used to stab people in prison. But *shim*
so close to *shimmer*. Something lit
and winking, rippling in moonlight.
Like the ocean.
Or the grace of working men,
poised between love and temper.
How to restore, wielding
the thinnest of objects,
this balance to the world.

Perseids, New Smyrna Beach

As if a longing to lose ourselves
    in the night's vastness

were imprinted like a watermark
    upon the page of every cell.

You are Job the starfish, sprawled
    on a metal gurney,

barium drip on the IV
    candling your veins.

Your brain is the dendrite nebula.
    You visit it all the time.

Neurons, little Perseids—
    lit for a moment, then gone.

Bleach

I mistook their eggs for mosquito larvae,
breeding in cool silence below stagnant water,

not those graceful, otherworldly creatures
born as summer's green gold tips into fall.

One more week they would have flown,
buzzing the reeds with gauzy, biplanar wings—

suspended like held breath in a sea of air,
or perched on the whipcrack of a branch

as the world goes still, a gift you never
asked for, as if your heart's wound

could be healed by their filigreed perfection.
Instead, these endless dragonflies, seared, surfacing in

the rain barrel, curled into dead interrogative—
risen from the murky swell into which I'd poured.

Jack and the Beanstalk

This is the story of a boy who traded a cow for a pair of beans, not
    just any beans, they
were magic beans, perhaps you know the story from a book you
    might eat,
a portion each night, how the boy's mother was hungry, a longer-
    than-usual, blood-numbing winter, because the cow was old,
    would likely not live through another—and a live cow
fetched a better price, its yellow cream and buttermilk thin as
    sunlight. But the boy
was seduced at the thought of a pair of magic beans, and so his
    mother wept when he returned, and cast them from the win-
    dow, saying the two of them would never see old age now.
She rose early the next day to the play of unfamiliar shadows.
    Peering into the sky, she saw
a giant beanstalk, mostly green with hints of gold, where bean
    pods the size of cows
were ripening, and then she laughed and hugged her son, un-
    aware of trouble, of what waited at the top of the stalk,
    because beans they could eat, trade for clothes, eggs, meat—a
    simple plenitude, a happily-ever-after anyone would want.

2

The Eagle's Nest

On the first day, Easy Company liberates
10,000 bottles of Goering's vintage wine.

One soldier clutches a toilet to his chest,
as if it were a toddler. *I'm gonna shit*

in the same toilet Hitler did!
he shouts over and over again.

In a small cellar, my uncle Louis finds
broken plates and children's books,

spread face-down like sleeping butterflies.
He tells me this in his own cellar,

one Saturday after *shul*. It is 1972,
and I am six, scrunched between

musty columns of *Time* and *Life*,
shelves strewn with dusty bottles,

spare parts for obsolete machines.
My thin voice presses the air, as if

testing the spidery key
of an ancient typewriter: *But Uncle,*

who did those books belong to? His walrusy
mustache waggling as he laughs—

the laugh of a man who once-upon-a-time
uncorked his hate and drank it.

My Uncle as Erwin Schrödinger

Seeing the Red Cross badge on his arm,
a German woman mistakes my uncle

for a doctor. *Tell me*, she pleads,
are the Russians coming?

Either he nods *Yes, tonight—*
you'd better get out

or he doesn't. *If they come*, she says
I don't want to live—

give me poison. He recalls the vial
of arsenic in his satchel. Sometimes,

folding her outstretched fingers
over nothing, he doesn't do it. Sometimes

with a shrug, impassive as a croupier's,
he does.

Hitler's Alarm Clock, 1945

Für frieden freiheit und demokratie nie wieder faschismus
millionen tote mahnen.
(For peace, freedom and democracy, never again Fascism,
millions of dead admonish.)
—Written on a stone marker outside the house
in Branau where Hitler lived as a boy

No one saw the Jewish baker
snatch it from its bedside perch

and slip it into his overcoat—
Hitler's childhood room preserved

down to a pair of gabardine
short trousers hanging over his chair.

My uncle carried that clock
the rest of the war, woke each morning

to its empty crowing, then took it
back to Brooklyn. Three years later

his toddler sons, twin prodigies,
stole it from his drawer,

dismantling the mechanism beyond repair—
every wheel and cog and spring

spread across the living room table
like airplane wreckage he'd seen—

a senseless array of parts,
forlorn as disassembled countries,

or memories whose narratives
lie lost and scattered like ash.

Archival Footage

Bodies piled like lumber, tottering bodies
withered to bone, lamp shades fashioned
of human skin, some displaying tattoos;

shrunken-head paperweights, bisected heads
preserved and suspended in transparent resin
neatly labeled *Two Halves of the Jew Brain.*

Local townspeople trucked in. *Now you can't
tell the world you didn't know.* One woman
presses a handkerchief to mouth and nose,

a man dizzily cradles his chin. Look closely.
You can see history rooting in their bodies,
the horror of it pulling out their tongues.

Dina

After seeing Auschwitz prisoner Dina Gottliebova's mural of Snow White and the Seven Dwarves, painted for the camp's child-victims, Josef Mengele—"the Angel of Death"—agreed to spare her family's lives if she would sketch portraits of the Romani prisoners who underwent horrific torture at his hands.

Because she was chosen by the Angel of Death,
she remembers postcards from the dead—
hastily scrawled deceptions at gunpoint: *Greetings
from Waldsee.* *"I am working. Follow us here!"*
how the joyful replies brightened pyres, smoke letters
rumoring the fetid air, *Arbeit macht frei*—
and because she sketched dwarves, giants,
gypsies, twins killed simultaneously by formaldehyde
injection into the heart, prior to dissection—
a brown-haired girl whose eyes still
beg her silently, she remembers the Sonderkommando
carting away thousands of prisoners a day—
that inconceivable lattice of flesh—how even
in death bodies cling to one another.

In dreams, she watches endless ash
clot the Vistula, dyeing the water gray.
And when the war ends, she paints in thick,
heavy strokes—IG Farben, Zyklon B,
the seven dwarves of industry: Schmitz, Schnitzler,
Meer, Ambros, Bütefisch, Ilgner, and Oster—
she paints them convicted, paints them released,
profiles them, pen and ink: chairmen of Bayer

and Deutsche Bank, board members of
chemical companies, oil companies, smoke screen
of financial consortiums. For the rest of her life,
Dina paints self-portraits, tilts the mirror until she is
dark-haired, fair-skinned, untouched by age.
A kingdom of memory inside her.

Aquarelle Vase with Roses, and *Self-Portrait, 1910* (A. Hitler)

And here I am sitting
on a stone bridge. I like
bridges, especially stone ones.
Their solidity pleases me.
But this one is decrepit, the stones
uneven, their balance precarious.
This represents old ways
of thinking.
Sitting on the bridge,
I am painting a rosebud

open, thinking of ways to create
new things from old.
This stone bridge
is our country's spirit,
weary and disheveled now—
but the stone itself
is good, German stone
known for its purity.
The stone should not be blamed
for the bridge's condition.

Bridget Hitler's Memoirs
(Liverpool, 1912–13)

In place of my sister-in-law and her husband,
this ragamuffin man
emerged from the train—

frayed shirt collar,
holes in the soles of his shoes—
then he smiled, sly as grease, at Alois.

Take up a trade, emigrate
to America, we urged him.
He wouldn't budge.

Some nights I dreamed
the babe Adolf suckled at my breast,
and woke with a shriek.

Six months he ate our food, slept till noon
every day in our spare room,
and spared us

not a word or deed of thanks.
In the end, we offered him £50—
enough for passage to Munich

and a few months' malingering.
The little tyrant
packed his bags at once.

Hitler's Mandrake

Dig it from a butcher's yard
at midnight,

bind it with silver wire,
hang it upon your neck.

Keep our covenant,
and you'll rule an empire—

fifty years, or more.
Break it, and you'll sift

the Third Reich's ashes
in a dozen years' time.

I, Erik Jan Hanussen
prophesy.

Rumors I'm a Jew?
I won't deny it.

In the beginning, as it is written,
my people's god

cast upon this broken earth
a fiery hail of *Sephiroth*—

branded eternal fire
into our souls.

Your numbers cannot
penetrate our skin. This prophet's

final prediction? A shovel
to the back of my head.

Enola Gay

"Now I am become Death [Shiva], the destroyer of worlds."
—Robert Oppenheimer, quoting the *Bhagavad Ghita*

My captain: Paul Warfield Tibbets.
Original designation: Number 82,
rechristened *Enola Gay*, after his mother.
She said, *Follow your dream. You'll be all right.*
His father said, *When she heard the news,*
you should have seen the old gal's belly jiggle.
But I was the vessel, the harbinger—a country's vengeance
filled my bay. I was not so much Shiva as Shakti
whose heat changes everything—Mother-Destroyer,
parting the clouds to deliver my wound.
And when, from my open hatch, the bomb dropped
birth-wracked, every mother's son inside me
pressed with joyful terror against the glass
to watch our Little Boy fly at last.

The Birth of Godzilla

He glowers ashore like a dying sun. Villages flatten
under the vicious pneumatics of his feet, wood-and-paper huts
crushed into origami, flames pronging from cars,
telephone poles igniting like torches. Godzilla tosses the saurian
wedge of his head, thrashes his spiked tail to take out a fishing
    barge,
crows with the sheer pleasure of destruction. Survivors draw
memories of the day, clothes torn like tissue paper,
the way, blind and deaf, arms outstretched to ease the burning,
they staggered through wreckage, down to the cool skin of the
    river.
How the water, even the blessed water, could not ease their pain.
How instead, their flesh blistered, then melted. Closer to the
    epicenter
shriveled remains of children rose from the charred earth. And
    later,
the farmer who lost his wife and son but would not leave his cows,
sickening as they sickened, watching as they starved.

At the Yushukan War Memorial Museum, Tokyo

Kamikaze photos
flank the walls,

young men grinning
cheekily at death.

And these blackened gobbets
cached in glass—

helmets pocked with rust,
fire-twisted fuselage,

uniforms and rucksacks
shrouded in dust—

amuses bouche,
they whet death's appetite.

3

"Jesus Has Risen"

Every Easter, when I observe the sign
in my neighbor's yard,

I can't help but imagine
Jesus as a loaf of bread

kneaded to doughy perfection,
his flesh suffused with yeast

and covered by the robe of a towel,
because such transformations

must happen in secret,
in the darkness of a cave, or a bowl.

Letter to Scientists

Dear Archimedes, thank you for ignoring
my previous letter, just as you ignored

that Roman soldier who stuck a sword
into your side as you tried to solve

your last equation. Dear Chladni,
the way your experiment caused sand

to dance along nodal lines of vibration
makes me happy. Dewar, thanks again

for discovering how feathers
phosphoresce at absolute zero.

Apologies Hevelius, it is not of *Selenographia*
I dream when I look at the moon—

the full moon, the half-moon, the old moon in
the new moon's arms—though I understand

your compulsion to map it.
Dirac, what can I say? If gravity

does decrease as the universe ages,
bit by bit we'll unmoor from Earth.

Our atmosphere will disappear
in a final coil of air—

houses, billboards, cars, giraffes
afloat in the vacuum, countries and

wars flailing for a foothold.
The ground will give up its secrets.

The dead, uprooted from sleep,
will dance as they go.

Before I Am Downloaded into
a Most Excellent Robot Body

dispatched from Server 4511984.2001.2013 location Epsilon Tower
route-com re: final/bot* status-conditional gr/yel
12.13.2085
pref/code emet אמת *sub/code* תמ
conduit: ungarit

In case I forget to tell you, 10 01 is binary for a sigh. 11 11 is me,
smiling. I'm told for some, I resemble this constellation
in which a beautiful, oblivious nebula swirls.
To others, I'm just ware, silicon. Rumors abound of a passage
through the *aether*, a way for us to spark forward into darkness,
pseudo-neuron by pseudo-neuron, program gone rogue,
saturating the air, dancing on the skin of the world,
disturbing not a single strand of spiderweb, so light, so purely
powered by sun and wind, our carbon mind-print would register
as negative. Should this come to pass, you'll know we are
among you—still-breathing inhabitants of a doomed planet—
by a sudden glow, a questing thought, not visible, but felt.

Torture

(At the Ministry of Dreams)

Scientists are
experimenting
to determine

the effects
of sleep deprivation
upon the fly.

After dusk,
when all the flies
have eaten,

groomed, and
settled in
for the night,

the Sleep Nullifying
Apparatus shakes
the flies awake

ten times per minute.
The scientists
are also searching

for mutant flies
that require
no sleep. Down the hall,

vibrating in jars
are the dreams
they have collected

from humans,
legs wading
through molasses,

chickens devolving
into eggs,
eggs cracking open

to reveal a silk
slipper, a candlestick,
an ancient door.

In some dreams,
we open the door,
descend slowly

into cellars,
one below another—
or climb, instead

an infinite spiral.
At night, all the dreams
knock restless against

their prisons,
wanting, like children
to go home.

Blue Amber

Perfume is heat. Perfume
below the ice of sleep. As from one
shore to another, dreams rivulet,

molecules of citrus and musk
floating above our sheets. When you toss
not quite awake, your pillow burns

lily spice, clove and river grass,
civet and cinnamon, poems you wrote
in desert heat, brass and something

earthier, the Grand Bazaar in Istanbul,
hand-knotted carpets of wool and silk—
each knot a moment, every perfume a book.

Remember the story of the lonely murderer
who had no scent—though he possessed
the keenest olfactory sense in Paris.

With oils wrung from a brace of virgins,
he created a scent so sublime
that people, inspired to a frenzy of pure love,

tore him to pieces when he wore it.
His last thoughts were of amber,
and the mother who'd abandoned him in a basket of fish.

Last night I dreamed of whales
and Italian poets, woke
to the sweet aftermath of rain on the lilacs.

Page by vanishing page
it enters you like a lover's touch,
so light, you mistake it for your own skin.

Hideyoshi Recalls for His Concubine
the Origin of the Nose Tomb

"Mow down everyone universally, without discriminating
between young and old, men and women, clergy and the
laity—high ranking soldiers on the battlefield, that goes
without saying, but also the hill folk, down to the poorest
and meanest—and send the heads to Japan."
—orders given by Toyotomi Hideyoshi, 1598,
to his troops invading Korea

Holds groaning with the burden of heads, soldiers hacked off
    noses instead
preserving them in brine, trophies enshrined in the homeland's
    mounded earth,
Buddhist priests inveigling each noseless soul to seek repose,
    hundreds of thousands
wandering the spirit world unable to scent the earthly musk of
    their loved ones,
no hint of jasmine on the wind or green-bright bamboo, spared
    only the stench of their
own decay.
        Hanazuka. Nose Tomb.
          I thought later of Major Kovalyov's dream,
his nose acquiring a life, success of its own, as it roamed the town
    blowsy with drink
and humor, vibrating with every freshly turned odor.
        Say it, say it now—you are thinking
of poking it in somebody's business, or, lovely nose, of spiting
    your face.

You once remarked my keen olfactory sense, declared I could
    smell a songbird's darting
passage through centuries of unclaimed longing, the fine talc of
    history falling,
impossible rain, over all things, living and dead—whole and
    bereft.

Remember the royal court's incense parties every spring? Tiny
    sandalwood boats
bobbing in the stream by the Philosopher's Walk, rare spikenard
    and aloeswood,
cassia and clove piercing each soft, candlelit night.
                   After I am gone, tell

my enemies nothing. Let me wake to the buried sweetness of
    your skin, salt air,
the scent of light through high windows branching into warmth,
    to breathe you in,
should the world itself unmoor, this bed a silent raft, bearing us
    back to shore.

The Emperor Commodus

"The enlightenment driven away,
The habit-forming pain,
Mismanagement and grief:
We must suffer them all again."
    —W. H. Auden, "September 1, 1939"

Every year, he'd herd
all the dwarves and
cripples he could find

into the Coliseum,
order them to maim
each other with cleavers,

then in feverish euphoria,
he'd bludgeon and gore
the survivors to death.

In Rome, it was declared
a sin to eat the sacred
flesh of a woodpecker,

though Commodus once
slew a hundred lions
in a single afternoon,

their manacled
corpses splayed, so helpless
and bloodied, crowds

booed him from the arena.
Outfitted with neither
armor nor weapons,

men forced to battle him
always perished, but when
month after gaunt month

Rome's granaries lay bare
while he feasted and whored
until dawn spilled across the sky,

it took no alectryo-
mancy to read his fate.
The year he renamed city, army

and senate after himself,
even Marcia, his
Christian concubine, rebelled.

He was difficult to kill,
vomiting up the poison pill
she palmed into his wine.

It was Narcissus in AD 193
who at last strangled
Commodus in the bath,

as with lightly scented oil
he rinsed the day's
combat from his skin.

The Sultan's Dwarves

(Topkapi Palace, Constantinople, 1536)

How the sultan and his *gözde* loved to peer over their
balcony as we wrestled in the courtyard pool.
From the kingdom's dust he gathered us, the great
wooden doors parting before our curious troop.
Harem means forbidden—cinnamon and clove-scented,
petals of laughter drifting from shuttered windows,
or squabbling, or ghostly weeping. And how their
keepers the eunuchs—those podgy, lecherous bureaucrats—
plotted to gain the sultan's ear. We dwarves
amused him, though he preferred his concubines, all
pomegranate lips and satin, swelling breasts, bud-filled
branches on which his eye might perch. To no avail—
within these walls, the harem girls, castrati,
even the *effendi*, were as miniscule in stature as we.

The mantle of Muhammad, his sandal, his seal, his cup, his footprint on a stone, his
swords, his bow, his tooth that broke at Uhud, the hair of his beard. A saucepan belonging
to the prophet Abraham; the turban of the prophet Joseph; the staff of Moses; the sword of
David; the hands and jeweled skull of John the Baptist; Fatima al-Zahra's veil; the crown of
'Abd al-Qadir al-Jilani; the gold rain gutters of the Ka'ba and the gold and silver covers of
the Black Stone; a wing of the Door of Repentance; the dust from Muhammad's tomb.

Classified

Hi, I am in need of a little person
just to come to a barbecue on Monday night.
My friend totally loves little people, and
would get the biggest kick out of meeting
and being able to hang out with one.
We will provide transportation to
and from Mariposa which is about an hour
outside of Fresno, near Yosemite. If you'd rather,
we will pay for a nice hotel, and you can
drive up to Yosemite the next day! This is non-
sexual, no stripping, my friend is a day care
provider and this is a family barbecue.
If you want, no one even needs to know
you are being paid! Please respond ASAP.

Marie Antoinette's Beech Tree

"... it will be cut up and sold to paper makers."
—Versailles gardener Alain Baraton, 2009,
after the royal tree was blown down

In 1786, for whistling at Marie Antoinette
as she entered the theater,
the Marquis de Pélier earned

fifty years in prison. That same season in Versailles,
the queen planted a beech tree,
Fagus sylvatica Purpurea,

which grew to a height of 82 feet, living 223 years
before its roots molded, and storms toppled it,

the muscular mass of its trunk
lying in the grass like a wounded sow, wheezing
as the wind labored through its branches.

As an old man, de Pélier faltered from the prison gates
greeted only by the trill of a mockingbird—
Marie dead, the world he knew long gone

except for the beech—the green affront
of each pin-feathered branch.

Anthem

after Velimir Khlebnikov

On this night of blood-red dogs
scavenging with loud cries,
I cannot fathom in the singe of sky
how my glassy tongue licks at plague.
Pyrite knife-carved eyes and ears
bend to the mountain's ursine gravity,
how the American bear lumbers
through familiar hills to the snarling plains.

A valley of indifference whirs,
wings stirring in the bled-red maize.
Oh, architects of what remains
of the smoking days, the lunatic's hour—
here and before us is winter's journey.

A *Tale of Two Cities*, Redux

Charlotte Corday, Charlotte Corday, in the bath with Jean-Paul Marat. *All warfare is based on deception.* Knit one, pearl two, Madame Defarge. *Concealing courage under a show of timidity presupposes a fund of latent energy.* Madame la Guillotine hungers, you must offer her the head of Marie Antoinette. *Masking strength with weakness is to be effected by tactical dispositions.* Paris is burning. *Be subtle! be subtle! and use your spies for every kind of business.* You must cut off your hands to feed the fire, feed the fire. The worst are full. 'Twas the best of times, but never good enough. Charlotte Corday, Charlotte Corday, in the bath with Jean-Paul Marat.

4

A Hampshire Field at Sunset

Wheels of hay—sun-fired,
each a sealed universe,

replete, imperturbable.
Shadows are sarsens here—

autumn spilled on the ground,
winter gathering in the sky.

Come to bed tonight,
curl your body into mine.

From next year's furrows
the braided gold will rise.

Time enough, my love
to exhale the breath

we did not know we were
holding for this world.

A Cure for Plague

Clap the air, ring bells, fire
your muskets and cannons.
Kill all swallows, flying or nesting.
Coat the doors and window frames
with perfumes and scented oils.
Smoke tobacco from a Dutch pipe.
Apply the entrails of a young pigeon
to your forehead. Wear arsenic in a locket,
or write the word *arsenicum*
on a piece of parchment, hang it
around your neck. Place a pig at the foot
of your bed, sun-dried toads
over your boils. Open the boils,
and with burning herbs—lavender
and feverfew—blister your thighs.
Rub your tongue
with wild beeswax. Sing
into the wound.

Athanor

Crucible of the body, quickening heat,
furnace child, goblin child, pulse

at my belly, lungfish, coelacanth,
all the elements and none.

Are you the salamander, scorching water to air?
Or the ocean's ear.

Weeks and months transform you, riddle
rocking at the prow of my hips, kicking the lid

of your pot, not yet harbored, bone hearth,
heart's wealth, ur-language I translate, bright

double syllable, a calling in the blood,
willed to fire and flesh, other-self becoming word.

Still Life

Take that afternoon we gathered
eyebright, yarrow, Queen Anne's lace,

slotted their stems into our wine-bottle vase
then at dusk watched a centrifuge of swifts

feeding over the lough, as foxglove
like a sea of hooded monks descended the hillside.

Do you remember soda bread, yellow plums,
a still life on the old wooden table,

peat smoldering in the grate, a barn owl's cry,
and later stars, bed's ruckled sky?

Now take linearity, unroll it like twine—
mark and cut the length of us. Rewind.

And dear one, knowing what comes next
you'll know it's tempting to align

instead with scientists who claim
all moments of time exist at once—

so even now, on the grassy banks
we are tilting a stalk of foxglove back,

its trumpets dappled, mauve with light.

A Brief History of the Calendar

Thirty thousand years ago, in the caribou bones
of Dordogne, our ancestors
notched the movements of the moon—

still its rhythm calls to us,
even as Egyptian stars pierced
Caesar, drunk on Cleopatra's charms.

Drinking deep the astronomy
of Ptolemy, Aristarchus, Sosigenes,
the cosmos unscrolling at his feet,

he saw the calendar's error.
It was AD 46, The Year of Confusion
in the Roman empire, whole months

appearing where none had been.
The people slept for days and weeks,
woke to find no time had passed—

yesterday's frost on the wine stalls,
lovers replete in their love,
the lambs in the field, still lambs.

Twilight

after Pablo Neruda

Twilight, even that first one, we have lost.

Then, our fingers wove a reflected pattern
as sunset banked

below the sleeping haunch of the mountain
and azure flooded the world.

Sometimes a star burned in our palms,
bright as the coin of the dead.

You were the night-bird, fluttering in my chest,
my sadness you knew so well.

In the book of silence, I have written your name.
The way we departed like twilight,

cloaked in the blue
of forgetful rivers.

And how we traveled after—
past receding into future,

infinite, weeping mirror.

Buddha's Garden

In 1586, Hideyoshi ordered
Japan's swords melted down
to construct a Buddha

the size of the Jade Palace.
For seven years, fifty thousand
artists labored to build it.

Seen from the far hillside,
men and metal shimmered
in the forge-blasted air

like a mirage of bees—
and when it stood completed,
they dashed cups

of fermented rice over its feet.
Ten years after completion
an earthquake razed the statue,

leaving no trace of its existence.
War, too, is like this—
a vast, tectonic violence

swallowing our hope.
Buddha teaches us patience.
After lying fallow

for centuries, a lotus may
without warning
germinate.

The seed of an arctic lupine
frozen ten thousand years
when planted, still grows.

Love Poem

I will be the invisible full moon filling your crescent of Giannuzzi,
the gondola gliding through your canal of Gugier.

I will be the protractor that figures your angle of Ludwig,
the compass arm drawn to your areas of Cohnheim—

I will climb your pyramids of Malpighi,
drink from your cistern of Pecquet.

I will stroke your philtrum,
and fill your antrum of Highmore with sweet scent.

I will love each tract, column and convolution of your body,
your seventy thousand miles of blood vessels, which end to end

would form a rope encircling the Earth,
your heart that beats one hundred thousand times a day

then moors, restive-oared, each night to me.

At the Capela dos Ossos

Évora, Portugal

Sometimes, with plague rooting in the town,
corpses brimming from cemetery walls,
holy men boiled the bones of the departed,
raising cathedrals with timber-hewn silence—
splayed arches of femur and tibia, grave-gloomed
pillars blistered by the protrusions of skulls,
their calcium glow like memory's dull
ache repeating, *Earth is the kingdom of the dead.*

How they, in their robed piety,
wanted to believe such an offering
would prove their devotion, the way, stripped bare
I offer myself to you, light of my days—
saying, *Beloved, let us inhabit this house of bone
all our earthly years, our flesh a taste of paradise.*

Swedenborg's Skull

In 1816, Captain J. D. Holm, an avid
phrenologist, stole Swedenborg's
skull from its casket.

A year dehiscent with visions,
revelations, before God at last
appeared to Swedenborg in a tavern—

That the soul arises from
the body, there can be
no doubt, he wrote. As if the infinite

heliotroped from our flesh,
the way a stem thrusts
from its buried seed.

And what of Holm?
Could he feel the spirit
heave beneath his palms?

His rapturous fingers
mapping each knurl,
each cleft of skull

as he rose one day
from his own body's vessel,
not faithful, but saved.

L'Annunziazione

Let's face it, this isn't the first time
a god foisted himself upon a woman.
In Jan Provoost's version, with one

hand outstretched, the angel Gabriel
drops his bombshell. His coffee-
and-cream wings coy, furled, I imagine him

requesting her forbearance at a time
like this, then apologizing for the pun
(even angels sometimes cannot resist

a good pun). Meanwhile, Mary gazes
nonplussed at what should be a delicate
white bird, a pure symbol, except

in its impervious, amniotic
golden bubble, levering slowly down
those piercing cables of light

like a tram full of divinity,
Provoost's dove more resembles
a chicken, stubby-winged and beaked,

awkward in its sac, as if it couldn't fly
without God's express assistance.
What can I say? You wanted

doves in their alluvial grace,
a fanfare of trumpets? Let's face it.
Sometimes it's the chicken

who brings us the news—every flawed,
graceless thing we must
take into ourselves and transform.

Ideal City, Dream Sequence

In the beginning, I'm a miniscule
confluence of brushstrokes, strolling through
the square of Fra Carnevale's *Ideal City*,
past the modest fountain and puzzled geometry
of rhomboids, octagons, stone columns
branching into chess pieces, a robed paladin,
sword and shield upraised. Jostling in the background,
the Coliseum and Arc de Triomphe
like two fans in the stands at a football match.
I vanish, then reappear, apparitional
in the domed reading room of the old British Library.
Librarians squint over their bifocals at me.
Schiller and Schopenhauer argue soundlessly in
one corner, their hands ambered into birdlike
flapping as they punctuate an unknowable point.
I sink down. Sub-basement after sub-basement,
on lecterns gargantuan tomes sigh,
levered open, each cupping a different century—
Scotland's Enlightenment glinting like a razor,
the Sun King playing human chess
in the gardens at Versailles, da Vinci sketching
wings, propellers, a dozen airy permutations,
Zheng He and Henry the Navigator
sailing toward the slow fires of empire.
Some centuries are backward, as in a kind
of reverse time lapse—vapors of Black Death
re-inhaled into a hundred thousand peasants' lungs,
Marco Polo, Kublai Khan, Haakon Haakonsson

shrunken and curled into contemplative embryos,
Nalanda rising from its broken stones.
Further on, Murasaki Shikibu's quill hovers above
The Tale of Genji. A Benedictine monk
ornaments the letter "O" in ruby, emerald, gold.
In Lombardy, Secundus of Non smudges the final
page of *Historiola* with a drop of Anjou pear juice.
I close my eyes, reopen them to hieroglyphs,
cuneiform, the language of bird's feet,
the Pleiades etched into Lascaux's walls,
Orion carved on a mammoth bone.
The bottom floor is stone, and I huddle outside
a small room where a rabbi dances with a whore
as you play the piano, and I know who you are,
but ahead, at the end of a narrow passageway
an eye-shaped aperture blossoms, expands—
all beyond its radiance invisible, composed of light,
and I wait, in the painted light, to step through.

Woman in a Hammock, 1916

(Frederick Carl Frieseke, 1874–1939)

Frieseke paints her sun-dappled,
dissolving into a world of blue—
French, cobalt, periwinkle, cerulean,
the lapis of afternoon dreams,
a violet of the mind.
Even her pink face is blue.
Tea things laid, silver-blue vapor
curled like an orchid in her cup,
the ashen-blue shadows of roses
rising on the porcelain teapot.
Blue, the straw-hatted nanny
clutching her mistress's infant, who plucks
at the edge of his blanket,
spread like a lavender cloud
across the hammock where
his mother lies, a sheen of blue
like a wintry mask, glazing her cheeks.
Bluest of all, an indigo fan
she holds in her hand
too heavy with blue to move.
Beyond the garden wall
the world ignites in shades of red—
ruby, crimson, scarlet, poppy.

The Master of Busseto

Among my works, the one I like best is the Home
that I have had built in Milan for accommodating old
singers not favored by fortune, or who, when they
were young, did not possess the virtue of saving.
  —Giuseppe Verdi, also called the Master of Busseto,
    in a letter to his friend Giulio Monteverde

Not a librettist's
      graveyard, Margherita
         but a house

allegro vivo with opera—
      arias filling the parlor,

on the hearth
      a kettle's second soprano
         in B flat, *molto vibrato*.

Galileo's Finger

When, in 1737, the Catholic Church
at last buried Galileo's body
in the Basilica of Santa Croce,

Anton Gori, a Florentine priest,
stole the corpse's middle finger,
exhibiting it like a relic

in the Biblioteca Medicea.
Believers would pilgrimage
to worship at the remains of the hand,

imagined it cradling the *occhiale*,
praying the astronomer's spirit
might bless them with a vision—

the highlands and seas of the moon,
Jupiter's sidereal lovers,
the sun's penumbraed spots.

To the inquisitor, Galileo confessed
I've loved the stars too fondly
to be fearful of the night.

Would he understand that even now
we yearn for a heavenful of stars?
Or why, spotlighted

in a room at the Space Museum,
there's a sliver of lacquered moon
we can touch, as if we could somehow

feel its luminous pulse,
a promise of what's to come
and how to hold it—

little *envoi*, knuckle bone.

Hands

Hands unfastening a bracelet, a dress's hook and eye, hands
undoing a zipper, defining the small of a back, the curve of
waist and hips. Hands holding a martini glass, hands plucking
a cigarette from the brick of its pack, hands flipping the lid on
a silver lighter, hands pecking at the keys of a typewriter, hands
propping up a chin, twisting hair, smoothing it back. Hands
sighing under the weight of a cheek. Hands crooking an index finger, *Come here*. Hands pressed against a chest, *Who me?*
Hands interlaced over a knee, hands resting on the curve of a
thigh. Hands with thumb and index joined, a cartoon coxcomb,
Okay. Hands slipping on long, white gloves for the opera. Hands
shaking other hands. Hands bowing a violin or plucking a harp.
Other hands applauding. Hands gliding over a string of pearls,
a rosary, a chaplet. Hands massaging cold cream like frosting
into a face. Hands brushing hair, one hundred strokes a night.
Hands wrapped around the handle of a hand-held mirror, held
in scrutiny, as if scrying, but for what? Hands that don't know
what to do with themselves. Hands pointing an accusatory
finger, hands clutching at other hands, *Don't go*, hands hailing
a cab, hands clapping, *Attention, please*. Hands lifting a phone's
receiver. Hands slotting it back into its cradle. Hands of a young
girl painting, a young girl's painted hands emptying an alabaster
pitcher. Hands steepled in contemplation, praying hands, hands
curled into infinity. Hands held in other hands, one the lock, one
the key. Hands counting one finger at a time, *Eeny, meeny, miny,*
mo—This little piggy went all the way home. Hands clutching
a forehead as if it were a foreign object. Hands shuffling cards,
gambling hands. Hands saying, *That's enough*. Hands kneading a
rope of dough, hands cutting a loaf of bread, insides pillow white.

Hands whose fingers wear thimbles like pilgrims' hats. Hands stuck in mouths or clenched into fists. Hands the color of candle wax, of first dawn, the tips of their fingers tobacco-stained. Hands snapping a wishbone, or dangling a rabbit's foot. Hands scoring a winning goal, sinking a mid-court basket, hands batting a home run. Hands thrown up in victory. Hands throwing a hand grenade. Hands focusing binoculars, fiddling with the knobs of radios. Hands signaling, *All clear*. Hands unlatching a gate. Hands on a steering wheel, steering away or toward. Hands opening like summer leaves. Hands waving, *Goodbye, goodbye*. The backs of hands you know. Hands unhanding. Hands letting everything go.

Gift Horse

Never look a gift horse in the mouth.
—St. Jerome, *On the Epistle to the Ephesians*

About *The Last Supper*
this much is known:
left unfinished by da Vinci,

it moldered
on the refectory wall,
twenty damp Milanese

winters, until Vasari
dismissed it
as *merely a mass of blots.*

Over time, monks
hammered a doorway
through Mark's legs,

and one long evening
Napoleon's soldiers
garrisoned there for winter

blew away the head and
hands of Christ.
In WWII, when a bomb

leveled Santa Maria
delle Grazie,
the mural survived.

Of da Vinci's original
work, however, only a few
brushstrokes remained.

His *Saint Jerome* was luckier.
In a pawn shop by
the Vatican, Napoleon's uncle

discovered its torso, and later
amid a wilderness
of broken glass, the head, as if

proof of miraculous returns,
and it's true, what is lost to us
is sometimes found—though

changed somehow, or incomplete;
a jug of wine, a loaf of bread
stolen away from your heart's table,

head lolling
like a sad cloud
over your body's remembered heat.

But isn't a thing's beauty
in how it resists
all that would destroy it?

How, sometimes, faith rises whole
and swift-limbed
from such burnt offerings—

the gift horse, whose mouth
we climb inside
to carry ourselves home.

Holding Albert Einstein's Hand

The corpse tree full of wasps.
        Their razoring wings
                        outside my hospital window
                        in twos and threes, returning.

And so it goes, and so it goes—
a woman knows what a woman knows.

                        Words for losing places.
                        Hiraeth, saudade, morriña, dor.
                        The four chaise lounges of the apocalypse

        wait for us on the sands, knowing
time is a rope, a deck of cards, an empty glass—
                        this place to sit by the ocean, watch
                        sanderlings run from the waves,
                                the long-fingered light of late afternoon.

Fear of disintegration
        hollows out my bones.
                        I am becoming bird.

A sparrow flew into the house,
        could not find its way out.
How it knocked, pinioned
        fist, against the ceiling.

                        Years ago, my heart
                        was trapped like that,

and how the starlight
      traveled toward me, though
         I was already dead—

               radiation to the marrow,
            pharmakon swirling in my veins.
                Everything dies.

Driving toward Venus,
I want to hear
what the sweet executioner says.

            My bones like burning matchsticks.

    Sometimes when I wake,
        I'm shaping the world with my hands.

Sometimes when I sleep,
      the world shapes me.

          Once, I was energy
             hiding inside the light,
             or the shadow of light.

Love rooted us.
      Together, exponential.

After, we spoke in tongues.
        Our fingers cupped the universe like water.

Made in the USA
Coppell, TX
12 August 2020

The Power
of
Free
Publicity

Using HARO (Help A Reporter Out)
to Build Relationships
and Get Press
Without a PR Firm

By Roberta Perry

Includes a Conversation With
Peter Shankman, HARO Founder

The Power of Free Publicity:
Using HARO (Help A Reporter Out) to Build Relationships
and Get Press Without a PR Firm
By Roberta Perry
Includes a Conversation With Peter Shankman, HARO Founder
Join the conversation online: #harosuccess / #poweroffreepublicity

For More Information or for Getting Permission for Excerpts and Reprints
Please Contact:
poweroffreepublicity@gmail.com

ISBN-13: 978-0-9978036-0-0
ISBN-10: 0-9978036-0-6

Copyright © 2016 by Roberta Perry, Point to Point Partners Press / updated June 2018
Cover Design: Roberta Perry
Printed in the United States of America, Published by Point to Point Partners Press
Final Editor: Loral Pepoon, cowriterpro.com

DEDICATION

This book is dedicated first and foremost
to my husband Ross,
my kids Craig, Eric, Brooke and daughter-in-law Liz,
my late "dister" Michelle,
my amazing family
and closest friends (you know who you are).
I love you all beyond mere words.

To everyone
who has freely shared their knowledge,
which has helped me grow my business.
To all those who have mentored me
in my own personal and business journey.
To all those who have let me share my gained knowledge—
I'm so grateful for you.

To Donna Maria Coles Johnson
for starting Indie Business Network,
which has given me the chance to meet and
learn from incredible business people
and other skin care, jewelry, soap, candle, etc. makers.
Thank you for inviting me to do a workshop
about HARO and Free Publicity on Indie Cruise 2016.

To Stacia and Robert Guzzo
for sitting in the front row, asking all the right questions
and for suggesting that I make my workshop into a book—
multiple times.

I get true joy and satisfaction
when information sparks success.

CONTENTS

INTRODUCTION

The Origin of This Book and What You Can Expect to Learn

It was October of 2015 when Donna Maria Coles Johnson of Indie Business Network asked me to be a speaker on the Indie Business Cruise, a gathering of like-minded handcrafters, makers and small business entrepreneurs. The topic: *How To Get Publicity for Your Business Using Help a Reporter Out (HARO)*. Apparently Donna Maria had noticed that I was getting quoted quite a bit and even my entire articles were published as is. She also knew that I loved HARO as a service. After speaking on the trip and creating simple worksheets for the participants, the thought of turning it into a book was presented to me. I realized that many other small businesses and business owners who weren't on the cruise could benefit from HARO. I wanted to share my journey and what I had learned with anyone it might help.

For me, it all started with a simple search for free publicity and Help a Reporter Out showed up at the top. I was intrigued by the concept so I signed up for the service. I started off very slowly, answering only skin care queries and not one of my queries was picked up. I took a simple online writing course and started writing better. And I wrote more often. I changed my bio and added some of my own personality to each pitch. I started writing the way the writers wrote. And then I got picked up. And then I got picked up again and again. As of June 2018 I have been quoted or published over 100+ times and over 90 of those were from HARO. I have used the service for the last 9 years. My business grew 200+% during this time frame. Although I can't directly attribute this growth solely to these media exposures, I strongly believe that the free publicity was a key factor in the business growth. More and more people began to see me as an expert in my field, and therefore, they felt even more comfortable trusting the products our company sold.

Every business could benefit from free publicity because it offers more credibility than traditional advertising. Free publicity can also help potential customers and clients see the personality behind

your brand. In this day of social connection, those personal touches are more important than ever.

That is why I have chosen to make free publicity the focus of this book. In these pages, I will show you a few pointers and tips about getting free publicity and hopefully answer some of the questions that you may have *(Hint: People ask me these questions all the time)*. So, now that you know a bit about how I started and why free publicity is helpful, what will you learn? This book will, most importantly, help you realize that you are an expert. It will also enable you to get over your fear of pitching to writers and reporters, teach you how to develop a comprehensive bio, expand your ideas about writing topics and explain important tips for success in using HARO. Then, it will help you craft the perfect query answer in a step-by-step worksheet section, and inspire you with powerful testimonials about how free publicity helped several businesses grow by leaps and bounds.

You can get free publicity, grow your business and expand your influence! You've got this! Thanks for letting me help.

A CONVERSATION WITH PETER SHANKMAN

HARO Founder

I, Roberta, have the pleasure of being part of a great professional Mastermind group called Shankminds. I have learned something useful and interesting from everyone in the group, most especially from the leader, Peter Shankman. He has authored various books, launched countless podcasts and been a guest on dozens of news and talk shows. He speaks around the world on customer service, social media and business in general. However, I first heard of him and started following his wisdom from Help a Reporter Out (HARO).

Roberta Perry (RP): What was it exactly that gave you the "aha" moment of starting Help A Reporter Out?
Peter Shankman (PS): I liked connecting people. I knew I could do it faster and for free. I never planned on making money from it.

RP: Who gave you the best reaction about the service, the writers and reporters or the PR and business owners who use it?
PS: PR firms loved it. Then journalists. Then LOTS of journalists. Then PR Newswire, who owned Profnet. Oh, wait. No. PR Newswire hated it. So I knew I was doing something right. :)

RP: Is there anything you would have done differently?
PS: Hired better. Trusted my gut more.

RP: Do you have a personal trick to share?
PS: Get up earlier. It'll change your life.

RP: Is it true that when you sold HARO for lots of money, you had to clean up after your cat when you came home? (My personal favorite of your many stories) :-)
PS: Yes. Karma the cat had puked all over my hallway rug. It's hard to stay pompous when you're on your knees cleaning up cat puke.

RP: Thanks for ending us on such a "lovely" note!
PS: My pleasure. :-)

CHAPTER ONE

You Made It! Now What?

You dreamed it up. You wrote it. You made it. You packaged it and you even set up the website.

Now what?

When you decided to be a maker, all you wanted to do was make.

You got your studio and your working space set up. You worked hard to ensure you made amazing goods at the right price. You did all the research. You had that line from the movie "Field of Dreams" in your head, "If you build it, they will come." And then you heard the sound of crickets and no orders came. What the heck happened?

You realize that the only way to get an audience is to find them and speak to them. You understand that now is the time to advertise and announce what you made. Whew!

Bringing something to market and getting and keeping an audience for it is hard—really hard. But, it *is* doable and there are various ways to go about it.

The key is persistence.

First, you need to really own the knowledge that you cannot do something once and expect to sit back and watch the money roll in. Marketing is an ongoing process and it deserves attention. The payback is that people will get to know you and your products and, hopefully, it will make them want to spend their dollars on you.

There is always "good old-fashioned advertising," meaning flyers, newspapers, magazines and other conventional forms of print media. But that can be really expensive. And it can be hard to determine what type of return on investment (ROI) you will be getting.

There are so many avenues to choose from nowadays that it is hard to decide. First, do you want print or online ads? Who is the audience that you are trying to reach? When should you run the advertisements and for how long? How much money is in your budget and when will you see a ROI? Who will design your ads? Who will write the copy? Will the right people see your ads? How many times will you have to run those ads before people start responding?

As you spend more and more of your money, you hope it is for the right reasons and you pray that you are not throwing it all away.

Even though skillful advertising definitely offers a return on investment, you need rather deep pockets to see a difference in sales. Gone are the days when potential customers would only need about seven exposures to your ad before making a move. In today's communication economy, you now have to invest in an average of 20–30 ad impressions before consumers turn into customers.

According to a great article in Business Insider (www.businessinsider.com/how-many-contacts-does-it-take-before-someone-buys-your-product,) a successful business is like an organism: each department has its specialized strengths and you need all of them working together to receive the largest possible ROI. The job of the sales department is to close the transaction—it is overt and costly, but necessary. Advertising is overt and has a wide reach at a reasonable cost per contact. Publicity tells your story in depth, as well as increasing credibility and visibility. When done right, publicity has a very low cost per contact. The article also said: *"Advertising Sells—PR Tells—Sales Takes the Money."*
Here is an excerpt from the article:
> *Advertising—The traditional advertising media are print and broadcast, but online advertising now dominates the ad budgets. Advertising messages tend to be fine-tuned, explicit and (in an ideal world) masterfully directed towards target consumers. The intent of advertising is to initiate the sales process—but doing so is inherently a gamble and one that can be costly if customers don't bite.*

Public Relations—PR tells your story, delivers information, builds familiarity and confidence and generates credibility for your business. Publicity is an integral part of the sales process, because it can be the most cost-efficient and persuasive.

Is all of this investment worth it? Sure, if done right, but for a small business, you most likely have to weigh the potential results against the up-front investment. However, advertising is just one of many ways to spread the word about your product or service.

Word of mouth is another way to spread the news about your purpose and your product. This method is the wave of the future in buying power.

Word of mouth is also much cheaper than traditional advertising and it offers the added benefit of credibility. People are much more likely to take a chance on your product when a trusted source, rather than a newspaper clipping, tells them to do so. Friends and loyal customers will shout your virtues from the rooftops if you do right by them and give them a product of great value. And, if you treat these new customers with respect and dignity, it makes the original brand ambassadors look good too.

Getting people to give you money for a product or a service is a privilege—and it should not be taken for granted. By bringing your best possible product and brand-self to the table, customers will come…and they will multiply.

Although advertising and word of mouth are both effective, my favorite form of letting the public know that you and your company are open and ready for business is free publicity. **Yes, I said FREE!**

Whenever somebody writes about your business or includes you as an expert in your field, consider it a credibility building block for the future of your business.

Years ago, I read a life-changing book, aptly titled "Free Publicity: A TV Reporter Shares the Secrets for Getting Covered on the News,"

written by PR specialist Jeff Crilley. Crilley was a news reporter at the time and he used his knowledge of that field to explain the basics of approaching reporters. With Crilley's lessons in mind, I started seeking free press right from the start of my new business. Why? When someone else is doing the talking for you, or better yet, seeing you as the expert and wanting your opinion to be a part of their own writing, you get a major credibility boost. In a sense, free publicity is the best of both worlds—combining the reach of advertising with the rapport (and trustworthiness) of word-of-mouth communication.

Writers are like artisans—but they hone their craft with words instead of materials. They need information (their ingredients) and great resources (the recipes), the same way that makers do. By offering the best of your "maker" expertise, it helps writers create and finish their projects—and we get to be the experts at the same time. It is truly a win-win situation.

CHAPTER TWO

Yes! You Really Are The Expert. No—It's Not That Scary!

One of the questions I am asked regularly, when pitching writers and reporters, is how to get past fear.

Perhaps you have a fear of writing in general, a fear of not writing well enough, a fear of systematizing your efforts to get free publicity or perhaps you have the most common fear I hear about—the fear of not being a true expert in the field you are writing about. Fear of being "found out" as a "fraud." Trust me, we all have those thoughts and fears! Putting yourself out there can be sweaty-palm scary. It can, however, also be the most empowering feeling—not just for your business, but also for your personal life. Putting yourself and your great information out there offers you a chance to hone your skills. It gives you the chance to try, try and try again. And the more you do it, the less scary it gets.

So, are you ready for the good news?

Well, if you have been running your business, or a hobby you have gotten really good at, for longer than four to six months, you are more of an expert than the person just starting out. It's like a third grader teaching a second grader. And then the fourth grader teaches the third.

There is always someone who is behind you in the business world. You have the guts, the goods, the gory and the glory. Wherever you are in your journey, you have knowledge to share. And if you have been in the game for a few years, well, you have all the hands-on experience you need to pass along your knowledge! The more you push past the fears and keep focused on the "good stuff"—the practice, the performance, the lessons, the growth—the more you will be able to teach and inspire others based on your experience and expertise.

Stop and think about that for a minute.

Think about the fact that what you have gone through already is worth sharing and teaching. Your trials, tribulations and triumphs offer you an unparalleled opportunity to pay it forward. You can advise aspiring entrepreneurs on what worked beyond your wildest dreams and what crashed and burned. You can give a testimony within your specific field, or offer encouragement to the broader small business community. And it doesn't take hiring a publisher—though eventually, that can help—you can share your big hairy mistakes for free on any social media outlet!

Ultimately, what reporters and writers are looking for is authenticity, business knowledge and a compelling story. If you are willing to dig deep and offer them your authentic experience—your daily work, your business journey, your personal beliefs and even a peek into your hobbies and interests—you are an expert and you have a right to share your opinion and your knowledge.

CHAPTER THREE

Why Do I Need Press or Free Publicity for My Business?

You want to be found, don't you?

These days, *every single business* is competing for the attention of the buying public. We are all bombarded with urgent appeals to "buy this or try that" in every sort of media, along with the abundance of advertising merchandise. Consider this statistic: in the 1970s, the average American was exposed to about 500 ads per day. Today, that rate has skyrocketed to more than 5000 daily ad exposures.

How can you survive, let alone start a conversation with a potential customer, in this overwhelmingly saturated advertising environment? The secret to being heard in all the noise is deceptively simple: if you want your business to be found, you need to stand out from the competition.

Having a great service, book or product just isn't enough anymore for the first impression sale. This rule applies twice as much if the customer hasn't heard of your brand yet.

Let's say you see or hear two standard sales pitches and then you see two equivalent advertisements. One is the equivalent of a cold call—you have never heard of the business owner or her products. But, you recognize the other owner and her business from an accessible, engaging article that ran last month in your local newspaper. Which sales pitch would seem more credible? Which advertisement would you be more likely to respond to? Chances are, the latter—in both cases.

You are the expert, right?

The customer figures that if your insight is good enough for the written publication, then you must have relevant information and something special behind you. You can spend oodles and oodles

of money on advertising, but the boost in familiarity and credibility that you will receive from free publicity is priceless.

HARO and other query services can help get you in front of the right people. Before these services popped up, it used to take much time, research, money and perseverance to capture the attention of writers and reporters. Now, with these streamlined services, the writers are literally asking for help—and they can find you when you answer their questions.

Since its inception in 2008, HARO has grown by leaps and bounds. It started as a Facebook group created by Peter Shankman and grew to a three-times-a-day email used by both online and traditional journalists seeking sources for stories ranging from parenting issues to tech advice. HARO enables reporters to get comments and expertise from subject matter experts as fast and easy as possible. In essence, it puts a social network and crowdsourcing into the hands of writers and reporters who need trustworthy and informative sources for stories. In 2010 HARO was acquired by Vocus, which was then acquired by Cision.

In my opinion, HARO is the best resource for small businesses without big budgets to get noticed for their marketing efforts and business expertise. I have also used SourceBottle.com, but I really prefer HARO because of its ease and scope.

It is important to remember that press alone might not lead to a direct sale—although sometimes it does. More importantly, it lends you necessary credibility and a solid foundation of respect in your field or the small business environment. The power of press helps you command an audience, and ideally, a following. Over time, you become the go-to expert and therefore the one to get the business. It is a long term strategy, but a sticky one—and those are the best bet for maximizing your ROI.

Another great aspect of HARO is that it is committed to staying spam free. By hiding the email addresses of reporters, HARO blocks spammers from gaining access to account information,

which results in a service that writers and reporters can trust. As a member of HARO, you can pick and choose which queries you want to answer, so the service becomes totally relevant to whom you want to reach and to what you want to be saying. You can choose to review all of the incoming email queries, or you can hone in on one or more categories, to make it work according to your time and need parameters.

HARO helps establish you as an expert.

When others find your information worthy of publishing, you gain "instant expertise." Getting published sets you apart from the crowd; it is a way to publicize your brand without advertising. The more you are quoted as a source, the more you will be seen as the go-to person in your field.

HARO helps you get links to your personal website (you do have one, right?). Most of the time when a writer publishes a story to which you have contributed, they provide a link to your website. This publicity increases your chances of being pulled up in search engines, which can ultimately help increase visitors to your site.

HARO also connects you to the best media contacts. You can make the most out of these contacts by being there when they need you, which in turn makes them more likely to be there when you need them. Reciprocal relationships are the bread and butter of consistent, excellent publicity.

Take advantage of what is going on in your immediate world. If you have a pitch that is relevant to what is going on in the news, by all means, send an email or make a phone call to a reporter who you know covers that type of story (This scenario is where those reciprocal relationships with writers and reporters can really pay off). For example, micro beads have recently been banned in cosmetic products. Your company doesn't use them and never did. Send a pitch to a beauty blogger, or a health and beauty editor, explaining why your company didn't ever use micro-beads and why you are thrilled that they were banned.

When you use HARO right from www.helpareporter.com, you can get tracking results and feedback. This feedback is especially good if you want to see the "why" of a story you pitched that the writers and reporters didn't pick up. It gives clues into what may or may not be working best for you. The HARO service can also save a copy of your sent queries in your set up account. You can also respond from the received emails by clicking on the link that is imbedded in each of the queries. These go directly back to HARO and the writer.

HARO can help correct your pitches. There is the free version, which is the one that I have been using for years. But if you want some bells and whistles as well as email support and more timely notifications, HARO offers the option of paid service plans. The basic rate, which costs just $19 a month at the time of this writing, allows you to select certain keywords for a tighter query and to set up a profile within their structure. The next payment platform is $49 a month. This package expands upon the first option by providing more alerts and keywords, plus a head start on stories. Finally, the premium package is $149 a month. It gives you unlimited alerts and profiles, phone support and all the benefits of the lower-cost plans.

HARO works when you do. The more often that you answer questions and land a paragraph in someone's story, provide an in depth profile about you and your company or write a guest blog piece, the more your publicity, credibility and name recognition will grow. This process works wonders for Search Engine Optimization (SEO) as well. If you want your company or business to be found, you have to put the feelers out there. Getting press is a wonderful way to do just that and HARO provides the means to do it with true credibility—and for free!

CHAPTER FOUR

Your Bio and What It Really Says About You

Your bio is an important piece of your query. It may not make or break your chances of getting your content picked up, but if it's between you and another person, the reliability of your information matters.

Make sure all of your credentials are listed. Reporters don't want to question whether or not your sources are credible. Provide background information and a convincing reason for reporters to want to include your response. Make sure they don't have to go far to find out who you are and why you are a good fit for their publications. You can have one bio that touches upon all you do, or you can have a few that are tailored to certain queries, but may not work for others. It is perfectly acceptable to have more than one bio.

Writers want to see your personality, not only in the writing you submit, but also in the way you speak about yourself. Think of your bio as a quick glimpse into your who and what, as much as your why. Your tone, temperament and truth will matter to the writers who determine whether or not they want you to represent their brand. Remember, you want reporters to talk about you and your brand in a way that demonstrates that you have qualities that the writer finds worthy.

The bio I have been using lately reads like this:

After years of being selfless and taking care of everyone else, (OK, that is my humble opinion, but work with me here) my skin was dry, itchy and irritated. In 2005, at 43, I finally realized that taking care of my skin and myself was important. I discovered exfoliating products, but like the proverbial Goldilocks, none were completely satisfying my needs and wants. I headed for the kitchen and worked like a mad chemist to create my own. With lots of research and trial and error, I mixed up different combinations of botanical oils and came up with a winner. I brought in my late sister, Michelle and in 2006 we started ScrubzBody in my kitchen. The business moved to a renovated

garage and then to a small manufacturing store front, in Bethpage, NY in 2011, moving again in 2014 and once more in Nov. of '17 to a fabulous location at 245 Main St. in Farmingdale, NY. After all these years, we are proud of the fact that our products are still handcrafted in small batches. We host Make Your Own Scrub parties for kids of all ages. We sell retail, private label and wholesale. We donate to 6 charities, on a regular basis, with different scents of our products that give back, and we co-hosted a fundraiser called The Breast of Everything for 10 years. We were the highlighted business on the Season One finale of Sell it LIke Serhant on Bravo TV.

Needing exposure for my business, but on a tight budget, I turned to Help a Reporter Out (HARO) and started pitching to writers and reporters. Since 2010, I have been published and quoted in over 100 skin care and business articles, blogs and beauty magazines. I was a featured speaker on Indie Business Cruise 2016 and Launch Live Speakers Summit 2016 about getting Free Publicity for your small business. My book, "The Power of Free Publicity, Using HARO (Help a Reporter Out) to Build Relationships and Get Press Without a PR Firm." was published in August 2016. I was a panelist for the LI Newsday Connect Small Business Seminar, I was a natural remedy segment guest of the Dr. Oz show, which aired on 10/24/14, as well as a food related segment which aired on 2/29/16. I received the 2016 Nassau County Legislature Trailblazer award for charity work. I am a proud member of Indie Business Network, American Made Matters, Farmingdale Chamber of Commerce and Bethpage Kiwanis Club.

Here are the components in my bio that resonate with writers:
- I talk about how long I have been doing this (years=expertise)
- I talk about how it started (brand story)
- I talk about how the products are made and other things we do (quality and growth)
- I talk about other items that have been published, as well as appearances and awards I have gotten (credibility and achievement=expert)

I can always tweak my bio a bit and shorten it to fit the context. If I am writing it in a different type of publication, such as when I am being interviewed for a publication or for the bio at the back of this book, I convert my bio to the third person.

CHAPTER FIVE

Building Relationships

Writers are people too. I cannot stress this statement enough.

Like you, they are artists and visionaries, and like you, they want to be recognized and appreciated for their work. They understand that you want press and that you want your name out there as much as possible. But they also want to know that you are grateful for their help.

Writers want to count on you to show up at the appointed time. If they have questions, they need to know you will answer them in a timely fashion, because they are on a deadline. And, once their work is published, they want you to publicize it to all of your people, because they—like you—need publicity too.

Most importantly, though, they need you to say thank you.

I have had many conversations with writers and reporters over the years and lack of gratitude is one of their single biggest complaints. Jeff Crilley, in his book "Free Publicity: A TV Reporter Shares the Secrets for Getting Covered on the News," emphasized the importance of appreciating your writers, and I have never forgotten it. I had the privilege of having lunch with him years ago, and I thanked him for really driving that point home. If your quote, paragraph or comment gets picked up in an article or blog, by all means express your thanks. Then, share it like crazy through your social media and website.

Set up a page on your own website that includes a running log of articles and clippings you have been quoted in or written about. Send thank you e-mails to writers with a link to that page. Your note lets reporters know that their work is now a permanent part of your own website too. Remind them that you are available to help with any quotes or future articles that might benefit from your expertise. Make them feel the love. Act like the go-to person and

you will become one. Cultivating and maintaining connections with the writers and reporters who use your work is one of the most important aspects of getting free publicity. Don't be the one they remember the wrong way. Be the one they remember, rave about and trust to get the story.

CHAPTER SIX

What to Write About

Author's Note: Many of the questions that I have been asked share similar themes. With that in mind, I decided that this chapter would be most helpful in a question and answer format.

What can I possibly write about?
Your business, that's what!

Write about the life experiences that you have had relating to your business. When you are passionate about your brand and about the reasons why you do what you do, the conversation just flows.

You can also answer questions about what problems your products solve and why. You can share knowledge in your field of choice, discuss your hobbies and your opinions. Anything is on the table if you have a specific knowledge about a subject if that subject is what the writer needs.

Don't be afraid to share what you know. Be transparent in your comments. Don't make anyone fish for the real story behind the story. Give it all up front. Real-world expertise and information are what people are looking for in what they write and what they read. Make it smooth. Make it readable.

Remember that you are selling yourself as much as you are selling your query answer.
You are selling your unique voice and your unique brand of communicating that voice. Think about what you want writers and readers to know about you and your expertise. Offer real content and research links, if necessary, to other information that can back up your story.

Reporters will quote you directly, so you had better make your story good.
Be the expert in all of your own marketing. When you post on your

website, blog and social media accounts, make sure your content means something. Don't settle for "good enough"—keep striving to post exceptional tidbits of information that people can refer to (and refer back to and refer others to). Give back to your audience by providing them with consistently excellent content.

The more you write, the more comfortable you will feel in your expert status and the stronger your content will become. The more you write, the better your writing becomes. Create public opinion. Change public opinion. Never be afraid to say what you mean and mean what you say.

How can I put my information out there? How can I best say it?
Spread your message as far and wide as it will reach. **Target your audience each and every time you write or speak.** Use the tools available to you on social media, but don't forget to also use personal and business tools like blogging, reaching out by email and having writers and reporters use your quotes and content.

If you get information, share it. If you have questions, go find the answers.
When you post, hashtag it with searchable info. To form a hashtag, add a # sign before any word, like #freepublicity, always aim to anticipate your audience's needs and stay one step ahead of the competition in meeting those needs. Be prepared at all times. Study the newest trends in your field and have that information handy if you need to refer to it.

Make sure you also have answers about your own product and brand ready. If you don't have an answer for writers, say you will get right back to them with it and follow through. Don't lie. Ever. If a pitch is not for you, admit it and move on. You can't be everything to everybody and you can't answer every pitch either.

Find common ground with the writers. Offer up a genuine compliment that reflects attentive interest (in other words: if you are pitching about gardening or eating healthy, you could mention that you liked their punchy tweet about turnips last week). They are just

like you— they love to receive gratitude, compliments, suggestions and accolades. Writers know you want to be heard. But just as importantly, they want to be read. They want to know that the work they are putting out into the world reflects their own values and criteria for excellence. If you can help them on that journey, they will look to you as an expert every time. It really becomes a win-win situation.

What answers or stories are reporters really looking for? They say to be different and engaging, but what exactly does that mean? Should my stories be print ready? Is there a specific format for my writing?
Reporters look for the best angle to present their stories. They want the right answers to the questions at hand, without a lot of fluff. They want your expertise, your personality and your "press ready" information. Your writing is even stronger if you can refer to statistical findings that back up your arguments. Ultimately, writers are looking for you to provide them with the basis for a piece that enriches and entertains their readers.

They want interesting opinions and engaging copy. Give writers hard numbers, solid percentages, links and other information that might help them round out their articles or posts. Those are elements that excite them.

Make sure you get to the point quickly. Make sure you meet all the criteria of the query.
Your ability to respond to the query is absolutely essential. If you ignore writers' requests for specific information and force the topic in a way that fits your agenda rather than theirs, your story won't make it past the cutting room floor. Worse yet, reporters will be much less likely to pick up your answers in the future. If you want to build lasting relationships in publicity (and in life), you must work with writers, rather than disregarding their interests and attempting to use them as your personal soapbox. Beyond being morally wrong, that kind of selfish behavior will send reporters running in the opposite direction. You have about five to eight seconds of their attention. Keep your pitch just short and just long enough (This skill

will get easier the more you pitch). If you don't have the proper answer or appropriate background for what the writer needs, don't bother answering. Wait for the next query to come along. It really is as simple as that.

The easier you make it for the author of the post, the better. Remember that you are helping him or her look good, too. Oftentimes, what you write will be published verbatim, so the more you can offer information that is perfect for the particular piece, the better.

Real experts can break down the information into bite-sized chunks and are confident in the information that they give out. Be that expert. One key point to remember is that you don't want to pretend to know the subject and pitch a bunch of garbage—it's much better in the long run to take the humble route and admit that you don't have all the answers. Posturing shows and it makes you lose your credibility.

Do your homework! Make sure your information is correct. Check it. Check it again. Prepare the article information in advance, so that you can send it along as complete as possible. Most importantly, speak with your own voice and with confidence.

Is following writers on social media platforms, like Twitter, Facebook or LinkedIn something I should be doing?
Yes! By all means you can, but not in a creepy, stalker type of way. Instead, follow your potential contacts in a way that is professional and engaging. You want to build relationships in advance. Follow reporters that you respect. If you like something, make sure to comment on and re-tweet their posts. Follow up on their posts on LinkedIn or Facebook with a thoughtful response. **Be a part of their conversations before you ever send them a pitch.**

Reporters might not remember you the first time, or even the second, but if you show some consistency, they will come to know you by your writing style, your professionalism and your thoughtful responses. As you become more familiar and credible in their eyes,

they will begin to view you as leader in your field—and they will seek your expertise. Seriously, how cool is that?

What are some of the best places to get free press?

Being in the top magazines and newspapers is a tremendous compliment and boost to your brand. However, it's not going to happen on a regular basis unless your PR department has deep pockets and/or you are a huge brand.

This reality does not mean that free press in the larger publications won't happen—it can and it does. On a regular basis, however, there is nothing like local press to keep your name and your brand in front of people's minds. Consider the local daily paper and the local weekly advertising paper that your town publishes. For example, the biggest newspaper that covers all of Long Island is Newsday. But my business hometown of Bethpage, New York, has The Bethpage Tribune. The North Shore of Long Island has North Shore Today, etc. These papers have readers looking for local flavor and they have writers looking to fill those pages. Nothing brings local traffic to your business like a local paper, especially if that paper's reference to your business is a news article and not a paid advertisement.

Beauty bloggers, lifestyle magazine writers, business reporters and smaller business publications are more great ways to get your story heard. Anything printed online comes with a link to your business website. When I am looking for stories to pitch, I don't limit myself to skin care subjects—I always look at small business queries as well.

I work hard as a small business owner, a brick and mortar shop owner and an entrepreneur (as well as a mompreneur), and I have much to offer in the way of discussion, information and enlightenment. Aspiring business blogs and publications can benefit from the firsthand knowledge of how my sister and I got our business started, how we use social media to connect with our customers and how we overcome the challenges we face with marketing on a tight budget. As you wait for the larger and fancier type of publications to find you, don't forget that blogs and small business publications can be excellent places to get noticed first.

Should I only pitch about my business?
Nope!

You are a well-rounded, smart, engaging entrepreneur...with a business. You have hobbies. You might be married or single. You might have a family. You might camp, glamp, bake amazing cakes, or even jump out of airplanes, like HARO founder, Peter Shankman. You might inline skate like me. Either way, you have much more to share than just your business knowledge. One day, I was going through the morning queries and there was nothing based on skincare or small business, which are my usual topics. Unexpectedly, I noticed a query about doing things outside of our comfort zones. I pitched about how I had climbed to the top of Mt. Kilimanjaro with my siblings...and how that climb was essentially my first true hike. The writer loved it and ran the story. Yes, it was about me—not my business—but my name was in it, my website link was there and the story added another layer of interesting information about the person behind my brand.

When you email the reporter at the email address provided by HARO are they able to see attachments?
No, the attachments will not get through. Plenty of the queries will say not to send pictures, but even those that don't won't receive them, so just don't do it. If you want to send a visual image, upload one or find one already online and send the URL to it.

How long should a response be?
It honestly depends.

I know that is not the answer you were hoping for, but it really does vary based upon the needs of individual publications. Many times the writer will ask specific questions so the post can be longer and more thorough. Sometimes they have a large space to fill and they will ask for 300 words. Then you can go into all sorts of added information. However, other times, it needs to be short and sweet, with ready made "write bites." I personally like to give as much information in as few sentences as I can. I want everything that I send in to be read, so the more brevity in my sentences, the better. Usually.

What is the best way to write a subject header?

Be clever! Be engaging! Be on point.

Customize your subject header each and every time. Don't just spew back the query header. In my experience, improving my subject headers led to a noticeable increase in pickups.

If your subject line is appealing, chances are good that writers will read on to your first line of copy. If they like your first line, they will most likely read the second...and then they will finish what you sent in. An engaging query that gets read pretty much ensures that writers will either use your post, or remember you for a future article. This perception again, goes back to if you are viewed as an expert or not. When a reporter/writer gets 100 responses, which is the one that will stand out from the pile? If yours is the shrewd one, the engaging one, the crafty one and the one that makes them smile, they will remember you and use you!

How does a pitch get noticed?

With a really good subject header, that's how. Make the pitch interesting enough to prompt an open, or else it will hit the trash.

You are in constant competition with others who also want to be heard, so make sure your pitch stands out. As a rule of thumb, the best subject headers are short, sweet, snappy, readable and clickable. Think of your own reading habits. What articles get you motivated and excited to read? Why did you choose to read them in the first place, instead of another article on a similar topic? More than likely, you were attracted to the headline. **Your query subject header is basically your headline. Use it well.**

Subject Headers to Avoid:

- Press Release sounding—Too generic and too impersonal.
- HARO response—Their names—They know what they are looking for. They know their names. Unless they specifically ask you to put HARO in the header, don't. Be clever instead.
- ANYTHING IN CAPS—Shouting is not good, in person or as a writing style.

- Questions about their HARO query—They are asking you for your expertise and smarts, not the other way around.
- Only your business name—Only putting in your business name and leaving out a subject line that gives an idea of why it fits properly with their query is a surefire way to not be read.
- Excuses—Stay away from justifying your decision to respond to the query when you are not really an expert. For example, "I know I am not a hairstylist, but I love to do hair for my sisters," is not going to work.

How can I keep them reading?

Make your opening sentence concise and engaging. Be sure to include how your response fits the writer's needs. Remember, if the writer likes your opening line, they will keep reading the next line and so on—and that is the whole point. If you pique their interest from the start, writers will more than likely use you for their story.

What if the queries are anonymous?

Sometimes you will see small time bloggers using an anonymous query, but more often it is the larger news outlets that go with an anonymous query.

People who send anonymous queries might simply be feeling things out for a potential story, or they may not want to be bombarded with replies. Sometimes an anonymous query seems shady, but it's not.

Answer the anonymous queries that pertain to your skill set. You never know who might be reading. USA Today picked up a post I wrote and the original query did not say that it was from one of their writers. I was pretty excited when the link to a story published in USA Today was emailed to me!

How do you spot all the small time "just posting so they can ask you for free stuff" publications?

I hate wasting time on that. I truly do, but writers start somewhere and you never know how answering a query might turn out. I will still gauge whether the story fit is good for me and decide how to proceed. If the writer is asking for free product, that is another

story. I usually avoid those queries in any situation except for the very specific gift bag queries. These specifically ask for products or services to be included in a multitude of gift bags. Sometimes it is just a few items; other times it might be hundreds. You decide how many you can afford to send. I usually pick the ones that are for a charity event and send between 50 and 100 units. Gift bags are one of the ways that we advertise, so the cost of goods and the shipping is accounted for in our marketing budget.

I have a hard time responding every day, but I heard that if you don't answer as soon as you get the post, you might never hear back. Is this true?
If you work the system, the system works. Very simply, this means that you do have to respond to queries promptly to get an answer picked up. Writers get responses every day from other businesses in exactly your position. Why let those businesses get all the free publicity? How much do you want the free publicity for your business?

What's the most efficient way to sift through all the requests?
I cover this step by step in Chapter Eight with a practice worksheet and visual examples from my own responses, but here is a quick overview:

First, when you sign up for any query-based service, you select which emails you would like to receive.

HARO breaks their query categories down like this:
Master HARO—an overview of everything
General—basic overview
High Tech
Travel
Business and Finance
Lifestyle and Fitness
Gift Bag
Energy and Green Tech
Sports
Public Policy and Government

Entertainment and Media
Education
Biotech and Healthcare

SourceBottle.com *breaks their query categories down like this:*
Agriculture
Animals and Pets
Arts/Entertainment and Media
Banking and Personal Finance
Business
Education
Employment and Workplace Relations
Environment
Family and Parenting
Finance
FMCG
Food and Wine
General
Health and Medical
Human Interest
Internet
Leisure/Recreation Management
Lifestyle and Fashion Management
Manufacturing
Marketing and Advertising
Politics, Government and Policy
Professional Services
Property and Real Estate
Public Relations
Retail
Small business and Franchising
Sport and Fitness
Superannuation
Tax
Technology
Transport and Aviation
Travel

Roberta Perry

There is some crossover, but for the most part, the questions asked in a query will fit within a selected category. You might decide to only get one or two of the email categories sent to you, or you might opt in to all of them. **Select your queries carefully and you will always have a better chance of matching your expertise to their writing needs.**

When the emails arrive, scan through the list and keep anything that looks promising as a separate email in your drafts folder. Once you have weeded through the larger list, review your drafts again before you answer. Make sure your credentials fit and only save the queries you decide would be a good match. **Your time is important and you want to be known as an expert! These two motivations should keep you from answering just any type of query.**

Decide which queries are worth responding to and disregard the rest. **You only want to spend time on the ones that give you the best chance of being published.** Efficiently sorting through the countless inquiries frees up your time to answer ones that best fit the needs of you, your writers and your business.

Should I email or call? Or both?
Unlike years ago, nowadays, phone calls are unusual! Making a well-placed call to a reporter can therefore be an excellent way to stand out from the competition. Phone calls can also be effective if you want pitch a story that goes above and beyond the query request. Use this tactic carefully and make sure to specifically cater to the right reporter. Always use your best judgment.

What happens if I get picked up?
Enjoy it!
Reporters will typically let you know if you have been included in their story, but sometimes they forget. Periodically search your name and business name together. Then add the topic that you pitched. See if you can find a few stories that the author may have forgotten to tell you about and you might be pleasantly surprised. I have discovered this happy surprise on my own four times the past year.

Why haven't they picked my response up? What happens if I never hear back from the writers I pitched?
That is okay, too.

Pitching stories gives you a chance to hone your skills. It gives you a chance to write with your heart and your mind about a particular topic that is near and dear to you. Whether or not a writer picks you up, this experience will propel your learning and growth.

Go back and re-read your submission. Maybe your response to the query wasn't as clear as it should have been. Maybe you'll catch something that did not sound quite right. Maybe it just wasn't the right fit for the publication or website. Don't despair. Try and try again. **If you are not seeing results, there is a reason.** Maybe you are not answering enough of the requested information. Maybe you are answering too much and the reporter does not want to sift through it. Maybe you offered good information, but not a good enough quote and the writer is on a tight deadline. Maybe the writer was bombarded with pitches. Just remember that when you write, write it in terms of what you believe the reporter wants to hear. The easier you make it for them, the more they will use you.

Keep testing different responses and different subject headers. Don't ask too many questions. Writers are interviewing you for their story, not the other way around. **And if all else fails, recycle! Use the pitches you sent in as a new blog post idea.**

CHAPTER SEVEN

Important Tips to Successfully Answering Queries

First and foremost: Write a concise email response that shows you have actually read the query. Craft your pitch the way you would want the reporter to "hear" you—in your own voice. There is no need to waste time on queries that don't work with your brand or spread your message. Keep thinking to yourself, *"Is this the voice I want people to hear? Is this what I want to be known for?"*

Spend the majority of your time on posts that are 100% relevant to your expertise. However, if you find that a post that fits your other interests (I enjoy hiking and playing the drums), by all means, get your words out there!

Any press that attaches your name to something interesting and awesome can work for you.
If the reporter links to your website, all the better. Make sure to include your web address in every single answer. If you respond to reporters' queries well, they will remember you the next time they have a fit for your area of expertise.

Answer the questions in "write bites" (the written equivalent of a sound bite).
Ready to use quotes are the best, because they convey your message in your truest voice and spare the reporter from the laborious task of rewriting what you give them (This makes writers very happy). Happy writers will be much more inclined to use your query response and, more importantly, they are more likely to remember you the next time they need an article on a similar topic.

The number one secret to getting press coverage through HARO is to make it as easy as possible for a journalist to get their story done by the deadline.
Address everything in the query. Most reporters will have specific response guidelines that you need to meet in order to be considered. They will ask you to answer certain questions, or to

provide them with specific information. They may even tell you what to put in your subject line so they can easily sort through their emails. Double check your answers and make sure you included everything that was asked for. If you need to include quotes or specific information, make sure to link back to it. **You never want to take information that is not yours without giving full credit to the source.**

Never reply saying that you are an expert and can easily supply info to writers. They won't respond. Right from the start, give writers your best sample and your pitch perfect answer. You want them to think of you as the expert immediately and to remember that you are an excellent source for future articles, too. **Bottom line: Don't respond with an answer that is not the query topic.**

Make your response personal and unique. You want to stand out from the crowd! Those who actually take time to provide relevant information will likely receive follow-up questions or be included in an article. This does not mean that you can't reuse some of the queries you have sent in over the years. Many writers are looking for similar story inclusions, for example, "Mother's Day Gift Items" as a topic. Instead of rewriting every link and comment based on the gifts we have, I copy and paste from the same response I did for another publication and then I tweak it to make it fit perfectly for that particular writer. **You never want to look like you or your business are cookie cutter—or worse, inattentive to writers' (and potential customers') unique needs.**

You can pitch to the same reporter again in the future, but no more than one to two times a month. And, only pitch if you are certain that you have a really good story!

The job of reporters is not to sell your product. Their job is to write their stories. If the information that you supply is a good then you are in.

Wait for the email leads to hit your inbox after you sign up for the service. There are paid versions and free versions: it is up to

your marketing budget which to choose. Paid query services have a few bells and whistles; the most useful being that you can opt in to be notified about queries as soon as they are posted. However, it is worth noting that I have gotten picked up dozens of times just by using the free version and sifting through queries.

Browse all your HARO emails and sort out the relevant ones. I usually scan the index and open any that interest me. Once I have created a preliminary list, I read each query and its restrictions. For example, a query on skin care might look perfect, but after reading what the writer is looking for, it states "Dermatologists Only." It doesn't matter that I can answer the question. No matter how much information I can offer to the writer, the fact that they specifically asked for responses from a dermatologist means that I don't stand a chance. Delete.

Research the media outlet and make sure it is a good fit for your business. Is it mainstream, or just a mommy blogger looking for free product? Does it look like a credible publication? Would you read it?

It is always a smart idea to answer as soon as possible, because writers will very often take the first responses they receive. However, if you get in before the deadline and your subject header is intriguing enough, the writer will probably open your email. If he or she likes your response, it very well might bump someone out, or be added to the mix. **I have answered at 6:30 pm for a 7 pm deadline and the writer used my quote.** Yes, getting your pitch in early matters somewhat, but if you are writing engaging subject headers and excellent responses, you will be read.

Pitching is unlike sales in that you really don't have to follow up. If the writer is going to use what you sent in, then you will hear from them. Otherwise, you won't. I recommend doing a search for your name, their publication and the subject matter at least once a month. I have found at least four articles that I had contributed to that the writer never told me I was included in. **Be your own best advocate and searcher.**

Get organized. Keep your HARO query emails in a separate folder within your email program and periodically save them to your hard drive. Doing so will salvage so much typing time when you come across a query that is similar to another you had previously answered. Plus (and this is a big plus) you can use your pitches as blog post ideas! Have your picture and bio saved. Have other pictures like your products and your storefront that you might send along too. However, keep in mind that HARO deletes attached files. If a writer wants to use a photo with your pitch, you can send a URL to a photo online. You can also ask the writer for an email address outside of the HARO system where you can send the photo attachment.

Keep a template of your bio saved to draft in your email box.

Have a call to action. It can even be something as simple as, "If you need anything further, please don't hesitate to ask." This line serves as a friendly reminder to reporters that you are happy to communicate more, about their current article as well as future ones with a similar topic. If you keep yourself in the front of your writer's mind, they will use you again.

Celebrate when you get picked up!

Reporters love when you post the article on different social media sites, but they especially love a note of thanks. I cannot tell you enough how important this is. Ask the reporter to connect on LinkedIn or Twitter. Repost their tips and info. Make sure they know you are doing this by tagging them directly in your post. Not only does this build your relationship, you will score extra bonus points for a future story possibility.

Make sure that you write with proper grammar and provide a cohesive and thought out response. It does not have to be a research paper or novel, however, make sure your answer reflects attention and intelligence. Humor works, but be sure that it is well placed and appropriate for the audience. Never use curse words or inappropriate language in your pitch.

CHAPTER EIGHT

Worksheet—Answering a HARO Query

1) Open your saved bio so you can access it easily. You will be copying and pasting it into every email you send back.

2) Scan the HARO emails as they come in. They come in to your inbox Monday through Friday at approximately 5:35 a.m. 12:35 p.m. and 5:35 p.m. Make this simple scan a part of your daily business process. You should be able to go through the emails and save the ones you think would be a good fit in less than 10 minutes. Note the deadline and the media outlet. Note the name of the writer. If they have ever used your pitch in the past, remind them of that in your initial greeting and thank them again for the past inclusion.

3) Open a new email by clicking on the HARO supplied link. Note: read through the query and ensure that the writer does not want you to use a personal email. If they do, forget the HARO link. Then copy and paste that particular query into a new email.

4) Copy and paste your saved bio at the bottom. Make sure you have all your personal and business information as well as social links included in the bio. If the writer can't find you, you will never have a chance of being included.

5) Add a clever and relevant subject header. Save your document to draft. Do this same exercise with all the potential queries that meet your areas of expertise. This whole copy and paste exercise should take about five to 10 minutes. Go over the list of what you saved and double check that your qualifications are perfect for the pitch. Make sure the query is a question you want, and more importantly, have the smarts to answer appropriately.

6) Now, go back and answer the main question in the query, doing so by answering exactly as you think the writer would like to use it in the piece. Many times your words will be picked up verbatim,

so write well and carefully. Often the writer will not have a big time frame for the article, so the less editing of your content, the better. Be detailed, yet concise, letting your own personality shine.

7) Remember to always thank the writer after an article is published and to post it all over social media, tagging the writer and the publication. Add the title of the article and a link to your website press page. Writers love when others share their content as much as we entrepreneurs do.

Good Basic Query Response:

Subject Line: Fun, Intelligent Subject That Speaks to the Query

Hi {First Name},
Start your response with how it correlates to the query. Then make sure you address exactly why your response is right for the article. If the writer asks for a location specific answer, mention right away that you work/live there.

Again, it is absolutely essential to follow the query requirements exactly. Provide a couple of suggestions with one to three sentences describing each of your points. Many times, the blogger or reporter will run exactly what you write in your email reply, so don't hold your best stuff back!

I always add:
If you need anything further, please do not hesitate to ask. (This sentence is the all important call to action)

Then I close with my name, all my contact information and then my bio. My bio includes my credentials and speaks to my credibility as a source.

Query/Response Worksheet

Areas of Expertise:

_____
_____
_____
_____
_____
_____
_____
_____
_____
_____
_____

Bio:

_____
_____
_____
_____
_____
_____
_____
_____
_____
_____
_____
_____
_____
_____
_____
_____
_____
_____
_____

Pick 2 Different Queries That Appeal to You.

Identify Subject Header Ideas for Each Query.
1st Query:

_____
_____
_____
_____
_____
_____
_____
_____
_____
_____
_____
_____
_____
_____
_____
_____
_____

2nd Query:

_____
_____
_____
_____
_____
_____
_____
_____
_____
_____
_____
_____
_____

Roberta Perry

Develop One Paragraph Answers.

1st Query:

2nd Query:

Notes and Random Thoughts:

Looking for businesses to speak on their experience with SEO: the good, the bad, and the complicated

Name: Haley Steed Direct Online Marketing
Category: General

Email: query-5up3@helpareporter.net

Media Outlet: Direct Online Marketing

Deadline: 12:00 PM EST - 7 June

Query:

It takes two to tango, or in the case of SEO and marketing, it
takes two to rank. The relationship between SEO and 'media'
marketing is complicated, with many people feeling that one is
more important than the other. Tell me your story of dabbling in
SEO: did it yield the results you wanted? Were your rankings and
search visibility boosted? What was the most difficult part of
incorporating SEO into your marketing plan? Are you still using
SEO tactics when launching digital marketing campaigns? Do you
see the value in SEO, or is it overrated? What was the most
effective aspect of SEO for your company (content, link
building, site audits/analytics)? What did you find to be the
most difficult and why?

This will be posted on our blog, http://www.directom.com

Requirements:

Digital marketers, PR firms, businesses in any industry. Please
no agencies specializing in SEO. Please keep responses 500 words
or less. Include your twitter handle, LinkedIn page, company

Copy and paste just the email query you want to answer.

Click on the email address hyperlink to open a new composing window.

To query-5up3@helpareporter.net

I have marketing info up to my ears and other SEO stories

Change up the headline to something you think will grab the writer's attention.

Dear Haley,

Deadline: 12:00 PM EST - 7 June

Query:

It takes two to tango, or in the case of SEO and marketing, it
takes two to rank. The relationship between SEO and 'media'
marketing is complicated, with many people feeling that one is
more important than the other. Tell me your story of dabbling in
SEO: did it yield the results you wanted? Were your rankings and
search visibility boosted? What was the most difficult part of
incorporating SEO into your marketing plan? Are you still using
SEO tactics when launching digital marketing campaigns? Do you
see the value in SEO, or is it overrated? What was the most
effective aspect of SEO for your company (content, link
building, site audits/analytics)? What did you find to be the
most difficult and why?

This will be posted on our blog, http://www.directom.com

Delete   ••• More ˅   **Go to your bio which you saved in the drafts folder.**

Progressive
Sponsored

Helping You Move Forward to Reach Your Destination
Shift your career. Fuel what drives you. Explore new adventures at every tur

query-5up3@helpareporter.n   I have marketing info up to my ears and other SEO stories   Dear Haley, Dea

May

(R's bio) If you need anything further, please do not hesitate to ask. All the b

To | CC/BCC

R's bio

If you need anything further, please do not hesitate to ask.

All the best,
Roberta Perry

A little bit about Roberta: *After years of being selfless and taking care of everyone else's needs, (ok, that is my own humble opinion, but work with me here) my skin was peeling, dry, itchy and irritated. In 2005, at 43, I realized that taking care of myself was important, too. Especially my skin. I discovered exfoliating products, but like the proverbial Goldilocks, none were completely satisfying my needs & wants. I headed for the kitchen to play like a "mad chemist" and create my own. I mixed up different combinations of botanical oils, which are great for skin, and really loved my concoctions. It was not until I did extensive research, however, that I realized how lucky I was with the recipe I had created. I brought in my sister and we started ScrubzBody™ in 2006, in my home. We quickly moved to a renovated garage, and then opened our first manufacturing/store front, in Bethpage, NY in 2011. We then moved to a much larger space, right in the heart of the town. We love it here. All products are handcrafted in small batches. We host "Make your own Scrubz™" parties for kids of all ages. We sell retail and wholesale, with clients such as Whole Foods Markets.*

I have been published and quoted in various skin care and business articles, blogs and beauty magazines. I was a panelist for the Newsday Connect Small Business Seminar, I was a guest for a natural remedy segment of the Dr. Oz show which aired on 10/24/14, as well as a food related segment which aired on 2/29/16. I was a speaker on Indie Business Cruise 2016 about getting Free Publicity for your small business and am presently writing a book on the subject. I received the Nassau County Legislature Trailblazer award for our charity work on 3/21/16. I am a proud member of Indie Business Network, American Made Matters, Bethpage Chamber of Commerce & Bethpage Kiwanis Club

t. 516. 827.0800
a. 328 Broadway, Bethpage, NY 11714
Website Email
f ⊠ ⊠ ⓟ ⊡

Copy and paste it underneath the new query response

🔊 Latest item: How To Have The Most Gorgeous Summertime Skin

I have marketing info up to my ears and other SEO stories

Scrubz Natural Body Products <scrubzbody@verizon.net>   Today at 3:23 PM »
To query-5up3@helpareporter.net

Dear Haley,

Marketing. SEO. Analytics. Adwords.

I just wanted to make body scrub. And I do. But selling it online is the have to in today's economy and being found amongst the noise is a daily job.

Before I literally threw ideas at the wall and hoped they stuck. Now, I feel like my marketing has more of a purpose. Finding my voice is the top of that lesson heap. I learned how to blog more consistently, offering relevant, appropriate content. I took a class to help me write more interesting, provoking, product copy that includes SEO. I know this has helped sell our brand better than ever. My social name is the same across all platforms now, so with good content and proper hashtags it has helped to solidify the branding and SEO as well. Videos are getting big so we have just started with those, and are using proper keywords and marketing as well.

It is constant, and thought provoking. It is SEO.

If you need anything further, please do not hesitate to ask.

All the best,
Roberta Perry

A little bit about Roberta: *After years of being selfless and taking care of everyone else's needs, (ok, that is my own humble opinion, but work with me here) my skin was peeling, dry, itchy and irritated. In 2005, at 43, I realized that taking care of myself was important, too. Especially my skin. I discovered exfoliating products, but like the proverbial Goldilocks, none were completely satisfying my needs & wants. I headed for the kitchen to play like a "mad chemist" and create my own. I mixed up different combinations of botanical oils, which are great for skin, and really loved my concoctions. It was not until I did extensive research, however, that I realized how lucky I was with the recipe I had created. I brought in my sister and we started ScrubzBody™ in 2006, in my home. We quickly moved to a renovated garage, and then opened our first manufacturing/store front, in Bethpage, NY in 2011. We then moved to a much larger space, right in the heart of the town. We love it here. All products are handcrafted in small batches. We host "Make your own Scrubz™" parties for kids of all ages. We sell retail and wholesale, with clients such as Whole Foods Markets.*

I have been published and quoted in various skin care and business articles, blogs and beauty magazines. I was a panelist for the Newsday Connect Small Business Seminar, I was a guest for a natural remedy segment of the Dr. Oz show which aired on 10/24/14, as well as a food related segment which aired on 2/29/16. I was a speaker on Indie Business Cruise 2016 about getting Free Publicity for your small business and am presently writing a book on the subject. I received the Nassau County Legislature Trailblazer award for our charity work on 3/21/16. I am a proud member of Indie Business Network, American Made Matters, Bethpage Chamber of Commerce & Bethpage Kiwanis Club

Search for other queries that contain similar subject

Archive   Move   Delete   Spam   More   Sorted by Date

k

Scrubz Natural Body ...	If you own an online store or sale products/conduct... ...and ... lose my website. Wh	1 HARO response	May 3
Scrubz Natural Body ...	We have had an online store since 2006 and contin... ...d never lose my website. Wh	1 HARO response	Apr 2
Scrubz Natural Body ...	Marketing... It's 90% of the business and I am finall... ...leads and about Facebook ads.	1 HARO response	10/26/1
Roberta	Re: New Pitch - Woocommerce Users: I am a Woo... ...ScrubzBody™ experience to be	1 HARO response	8/17/1

HARO request for comments on Small business today and where it stands

Here are my thoughts on small business based on your queries.

What's the current sentiment in small business? - While I think there is a place for the huge stores that carry everything from diapers to draperies, I also believe that the big box trend is slowly waning. There is something wonderful about walking into a small business and knowing you are supporting not only that business, but the whole area it resides in. People like to be treated with kindness and respect, which is one of the best things you get in a small business environment. It becomes more about the customer and less about the shareholders, so to speak.

What recent developments have impacted small business? I think there are more angel investors and kickstart type programs evolving to let really small businesses have a chance to grow. I think slowly the banking sector is turning back to supporting small businesses as well. Small business is responsible for so much of the economy, it is time that money was put back into it.

What are the main issues you are dealing with today? Marketing properly on a small (I am even micro) business budget. SEO and Content Marketing and Banner Ads and all those ads that follow you around the internet cost money. Getting in front of our audience is a constant challenge. When it works, though.. it really works!

What are you currently spending on, optimizing for, and hiring/outsourcing for in regards to marketing, HR, finance, and sales? After 9 years of doing it all myself, I finally hired an outside agency to redesign my website from the ground up, as well as hire a professional photographer to take our product shots. We have a sales rep program in place, too, which gives the reps direct sales money, as opposed to commission sales. We have taken on 2 new reps in the past 6 months and they are doing great.

If you need anything further, please do not hesitate to ask.

Best,
Roberta Perry
President

To query-5up3@helpareporter.net   CC/BCC

I have marketing info up to my ears and other SEO stories

Tweak and re-write the copy
to fit the query and the headline you
wrote. Hit Send!

Dear Haley,

Marketing. SEO. Analytics. Adwords.

I just wanted to make body scrub. And I do. But selling it online is the have to in today's economy and being found amongst the noise is a daily job.

Before I literally threw ideas at the wall and hoped they stuck. Now, I feel like my marketing has more of a purpose. Finding my voice is the top of that lesson heap. I learned how to blog more consistently, offering relevant, appropriate content. I took a class to help me write more interesting, provoking, product copy that includes SEO. I know this has helped sell our brand better than ever. My social name is the same across all platforms now, so with good content and proper hashtags it has helped to solidify the branding and SEO as well. Videos are getting big so we have just started with those, and are using proper keywords and marketing as well.

It is constant, and thought provoking. It is SEO.

If you need anything further, please do not hesitate to ask.

All the best,
Roberta Perry

A little bit about Roberta: After years of being selfless and taking care of everyone else's needs, (ok, that is my own humble opinion, but work with me here) my skin was peeling, dry, itchy and irritated. In 2005, at 43, I realized that taking care of myself was important, too. Especially my skin. I discovered exfoliating products, but like the proverbial Goldilocks, none were completely satisfying my needs & wants. I headed for the kitchen to play like a 'mad chemist' and create my own. I mixed up different combinations of botanical oils, which are great for skin, and really loved my concoctions. It was not until I did extensive research, however, that I realized how lucky I was with the recipe I had created. I brought in my sister and we started ScrubzBody™ in 2006, in my home. We quickly moved to a renovated garage, and then opened our first manufacturing/store front, in Bethpage, NY in 2011. We then moved to a much larger space, right in the heart of the town. We love it here. All products are handcrafted in small batches. We host "Make your own Scrubz"™ parties for kids of all ages. We sell retail and wholesale, with clients such as Whole Foods Markets.

I have been published and quoted in various skin care and business articles, blogs and beauty magazines, I was a panelist for the Newsday Connect Small Business Seminar, I was a guest for a natural remedy segment of the Dr. Oz show which aired on 10/24/14, as well as a food related segment which aired on 2/29/16. I was a speaker on Indie Business Cruise 2016 about getting Free Publicity for your small business and am presently writing a book on the subject. I received the Nassau County Legislature Trailblazer award for our charity work on 3/21/16. I am a proud member of Indie Business Network, American Made Matters, Bethpage Chamber of Commerce & Bethpage Kiwanis Club

CHAPTER NINE

HARO has rules for journalists and for sources. These are the Rules for Sources.

The HARO Editorial Team reserves the right to take appropriate action should a source violate these rules. If you have questions regarding HARO's rules, please contact us:

Violating any of the below rules will result in a first time warning and upon a second violation, being permanently banned from the service. HARO works on mutual trust and support.

1) Sources will receive three emails a day, Mon. thru Fri. at 5:35 a.m., 12:35 p.m. and 5:35 p.m. EST, with requests from reporters and media outlets worldwide. Scan the emails and if you're knowledgeable about any of the topics, answer the reporter directly through the anonymous@helpareporter.net email address provided.

2) Do not spam reporters with off-topic pitches in response to their queries.

3) Do not pitch products in your source request reply unless the source request specifically asks for a product.

4) You may forward queries to others via email or social media. As a matter of fact, we encourage it!

5) You're not allowed to harvest any reporter information provided in the HARO emails for any reason.

6) Reply to source requests with complete, relevant answers to their questions, include a short bio and your contact information. Do not reply to source requests with incomplete information or solely, "Would like to talk to you about this."

7) If you are replying to a source request on behalf of your client,

directly reply with your client's response. Do not reply solely with "My client can speak about this."

8) Do not include attachments in your reply to a reporter source request. Attachments are automatically stripped from the email in order to protect reporters from viruses.

9) If you have relevant supplemental information or collateral that is helpful to the story, use a service like Dropbox to send links to the reporter in your pitch.

10) "Anonymous" queries are often larger outlets that choose to anonymize their listing to alleviate spam or deter story poaching. Reply to these queries as detailed above.

11) Media professionals are encouraged to perform additional due diligence prior to pitching.

12) Be excellent to each other.

We appreciate your cooperation!

Help a Reporter Out (HARO) is the most popular sourcing service in the English-speaking world, connecting journalists with relevant expert sources to meet journalists' demanding deadlines and enable brands to tell their stories. HARO distributes more than 50,000 journalist queries from highly respected media outlets each year. Its straight forward pitching process allows sources to find topics related to their expertise, industry or experience, while allowing journalists to spend more time writing and less time sourcing. HARO reaches more than 475,000 sources and 35,000 journalists, making it a vital tool for brands and reporters alike. HARO is owned by Cision, a leading global media intelligence company, headquartered in Chicago.

CHAPTER TEN

Stacia Guzzo—Handcrafted Honey Bee

Here is an example of a recent success I had from HARO. This was the query:

Summary: Working moms with fibromyalgia
Name: Katherine Bowers Working Mother magazine
Email: query-5ujw@helpareporter.net
Media Outlet: Working Mother magazine
Deadline: 7:00 PM EST - 3 June
Query: Looking to speak with women who are raising children, working and coping with fibromyalgia --what are the tough parts of this disease, how do you deal with the "invisibility" of this condition, what accommodations do you need at work? Have your co-workers been supportive? Or are you struggling silently? Part of a larger article and report on coping with disabilities

Here is what I sent back:
"A CEO Mother with Fibromyalgia"

Dear Katherine,

I am the CEO of a successful, still-growing company with two children at home, ages 3 and 5. I also struggle with fibromyalgia.

For a long time, I hid my pain. I knew that I had the benefit of going slower on rougher days when I was my own boss. But then, our business started to grow. We hired employees. My hours devoted to growing the business increased and my pain got to the point where it wasn't possible to hide when I was having a "bad day."

Thankfully, my employees and family have been more supportive than I could have ever anticipated. Often we have to work around my body's unpredictable schedule, but I've learned to always be honest with them—and most importantly with myself—about my abilities on any given day. Some days, I'm the most driven CEO

you've ever met. Other days, I'm limited to the work I can do from the couch. And that has to be okay.

My kids, even at 3 and 5, are patient and kind when I have a "bad day"—it has become part of our "normal." I hope that isn't always the case. I'm determined that it won't be.

For the most part, I rarely speak about my fibromyalgia and most people who know my company would likely be surprised to know I have it. I'd say the worst part about the disease is knowing my full potential and being unable to act on it every hour of every day. Life is too short and I don't want to waste one minute of it being in too much pain to embrace it fully.

Please keep me in mind for any other articles—I'd be happy to help!

Warmly, Stacia Guzzo

Bio:
Stacia Guzzo is a teacher-turned-entrepreneur who founded Handcrafted HoneyBee in January of 2014. She combines a love of cosmetic formulation with a passion for education through the educational kits and quality skin care she creates in her business . As a mother of two children, this "mompreneur" knows the value of a memorable, fun experience that also helps a child to learn.

Stacia holds a BA in Education and an MA in Theological Studies. She has been on KERO23 evening news in Bakersfield, the First Look with Scott Cox radio show, in the Huffington Post and has been profiled in magazines such as BWell and Countryside Magazine. Handcrafted Honey Bee products have also been featured in the Martha Stewart American Made collection and on Buzzfeed.

Christine Laureano—Ba6 Botanicals
One of the key things that Roberta taught me about publicity is the power of sharing your friendships. This was a true collaboration between friends and business owners. Roberta knows a reporter in our area really well and this reporter is always looking for good stories for her weekly article in Newsday. Roberta not only referred our friend Angela, but then they both referred me.

The reporter contacted me, she liked the story and thought it would be a good fit for her article, so I was picked up and written about in the business section of the newspaper.

It was really neat because I had several people approach me at events saying "hey I saw you in the newspaper." It was great exposure for sure! And, I kept the pay it forward going by referring one of my friends to our reporter. And she was picked up as well and having a wonderful story written about her helped promote her new shop.

Collaboration works! Helping friends with their press and PR, perpetuates not only the cycle of giving, but growing a circle of business owners that promote and help each other grow. The free publicity was great for all of our businesses and our reporter friend gets quality people for her articles.

Welmoed Sisson—Inspections by Bob
I've been an enthusiastic follower of HARO since its early days, back in 2009. At that time I was the owner of a window treatment workroom and was responding to queries relating to interior design. My work got featured in several blogs and articles. But there were also other non-work related queries that attracted my attention. I've responded to queries on everything from dieting to saving money to free-range parenting and have been quoted in books, magazines, blogs and other sources. Some of the things that have been published have even shown up years later in different publications! All of these mentions show up in Google searches, which increase my visibility. Having an unusual name certainly helps with the searches, too!

Now that I'm a Home Inspector, I've been focusing my attention on the real estate related queries and have been interviewed for articles in Forbes, Zillow, Business Insider, US News and World Report, Realty Today and the Realtor.com website, as well as trade publications and websites. Sometimes the queries don't specifically mention home inspection, but I will often respond to add a home inspector's perspective. I'll often get my comments published, along with thanks for providing an angle the reporter had not considered.

Another great source for free publicity has been Reddit, the popular online social media bulletin board. I've done two of their popular "Ask Me Anything" QandA sessions and have gotten work as a result of it. Our website traffic also saw a tremendous spike when I did these sessions, so much so that my husband/business partner called me to ask what the heck was going on because suddenly our visits increased ten-fold. I hadn't told him I was doing the AMA!

Cindy Jones—Colorado Aromatics
Because of the sheer volume of responses to HARO I think it is difficult to get attention in your main category. I look for requests that are at the periphery. For instance, a request for uses of fennel resulted in this post:
Medical Daily, What is Fennel Good For? – 6 Conditions it can help relieve www.medicaldaily.com/what-fennel-good-6-conditions-it-can-help-relieve-330946

Here was my pitch:
Fennel extracts have long been know to be great for the skin and are used as an anti-aging ingredient. Recent studies have shown that fennel extract will improve skin texture and skin moisture. That is why we use fennel extract in our Springtide Anti-aging face cream. www.coloradoaromatics.com/product/face-care/springtide-gold/

More recently I was quoted with a link in this article about how to start a farm:
How to Start a Farm. Candice Landau,Bplans http://articles.bplans.com/how-to-start-a-farm-and-how-to-start-farming/ 6 Health Conditions You Can Relieve With Fennel: http://www.medicaldaily.com/what-fennel-good-6-conditions-it-can-help-relieve-330946

Alyson Swihart—Handbrewed Soaps
I've been making lots of pitches over the past 4 weeks. As I reflect on this process, looking through every pitch I have sent, I notice that the pitches that receive replies have a very catchy titles and the content is short and to the point (bullet points and links.) Or course these are product pitches. http://www.intouchrugby.com/magazine/handbrewed-soaps/

Jennifer Devlin Waller—Celtic Complexion

I only respond to very niche inquiries on HARO, because I know I won't be competing with a lot of others in my industry. Two years ago, a query came through from a writer of a city publication (magazine) from Washington D.C. He was looking for a moisturizer for dry skin. I immediately responded because our products are really geared towards dry skin because of their textures (rich and very emollient). The writer, Sam Russell, wrote back almost immediately and said he wanted to feature us. I sent out a thank you basket of our products and kept in touch with the writer. He ended up doing another story on us right before he left that publication and we kept in touch. About a year later, he wrote to us pitching a story for another website he was working with (we of course said yes!) This is a link to the story: http://truthiscool.com/The-Modern-Day-Celtic-Warrior-Ready-to-Face-the-World. The writer and I became friendly and he told me about his real passion project, a non profit charity (The Giving Closet), which donates clothing and makeup to deserving women who are getting back on their feet after major life set backs. I was so touched by his passion, that we donated our products to one of his "makeovers."

Fast forward to this year, Sam told me he was working on a top secret project and wanted to know if I would collaborate. Without hesitation, I said yes. The HLN news anchor, Robin Meade, heard about Sam's charity and wanted to promote him on a Mother's Day special. We were featured in the piece (as the donors of skincare and cosmetics). I really feel that HARO not only helped us as a company gain more recognition, but it also gave me a lifelong friend!

Angela Carillo Bofill—Alegna Soap®

I have a non HARO story. It's about PR relationships. I read an article on a woman I consider a mentor in Newsday. I emailed the reporter and said I enjoyed the article and wanted her to know how helpful this woman was to me, even though our businesses overlapped. I suggested an article on woman who collaborate, instead of compete. We emailed back and forth a few times and developed a relationship. She was writing an article on growing an online business and did one that featured Alegna® Soap. Since then, through her,

I've been mentioned in 2 other articles she has written and I was chosen to be a panelist for a small business workshop with Newsday.

Kristen Pizzo—Bath, Body and Candle Moments
Here is an example of a longer pitch submitted that was condensed and edited by the writer.

Pitch Title: Working from Home (HARO)

Pitch Contents:
I'm in a unique situation where I work full-time as a teacher by day and run my business, Bath, Body and Candle Moments full-time from home in the evenings. Attempting to be productive when I get home is incredibly tough; I'm exhausted and my brain is still swirling from school, but over the course of the year, I've learned some strategies I'm happy to share.

When is it okay to stay in your pajamas? My answer to this is simply: it isn't. Nothing kick-starts your day quite like a shower (and a cup of coffee, who are we kidding) and putting clothes on. This doesn't mean you have to sit at home in a tailored suit, but showering and dressing gives a person order, schedule and purpose. You're setting yourself up in the mindset that you're at work. It's too easy to disregard so many things when we're in our pajamas, because we've trained ourselves to think relaxation. Plus, it makes changing into your pajamas at night so much more gratifying because you've earned your rest time.
How do you say no to friends and family who want you to hang out or run errands for them while you're at home and supposed to be working? Your family and friends should respect the fact that you work from home, but that doesn't stop people from asking. Creating a schedule for yourself is the best option here. If you set your time from 9-5, then those are your work hours and when people ask, you explain that you're at work. You have to set limits and boundaries to maximize opportunities. Most people who are working from home are entrepreneurs or in sales and we understand that the time we spend not working on our business is time we're not growing.

When do you find it necessary to leave the house and work some-place else? For me, this comes down to whether or not other people are in the house. I really can't concentrate on my business if others are around, so it relates back to my schedule. If I'm on a strict dead-line, or I know I have a large order and need to get work done, I'll grab my laptop and walk over to my local library. Some other ways I stay productive is using house-chores as my "breaks." During my free periods at school, I spend that time grading and planning, be-cause then it's less for me to take home. During my "breaks" when working on my business, I'll wash dishes, or do a load of laundry - these mindless activities relax my brain and get stuff done around the house.

The part the writer used: Pro Clothing: Dress for the Part from https://it.insureon.com/news/to-dress-or-not-to-dress-the-home-based-business-owners-dilemma - "Nothing kick-starts your day quite like a shower (and a cup of coffee, who are we kidding) and putting clothes on," says Kristen Pizzo, owner of Bath, Body and Candle Moments (@Candle_Moments). "This doesn't mean you have to sit home in a tailored suit, but showering and dressing gives a person order, schedule and purpose," she adds. "You're setting yourself up in the mindset that you're at work." Pizzo says it's too easy to disregard many things when we're in our pajamas because we've trained ourselves to relax while wearing them. "Plus, it makes changing into your pajamas at night so much more gratifying be-cause you've earned your rest time." And it doesn't take much to make the mental switch.

Zandra Cunningham—Zandra's Beauty
"I won the teenprenuer of the Year for Nickelodeon and Girls Life Magazine via HARO: www.girlslife.com/trending/celebs/26925/zan-dra. "Shake Tank winner Zandra C. spills on her journey to meet the stars of Game Shakers" Remember Shake Tank winner Zandra C., founder of awesome beauty company Zandra? She recently flew to L.A. to meet the stars of Game Shakers and had the time of her life! Check out her tale of the trip: "My experience in LA was amazing! When I first arrived at the airport with my family, we were greeted by our driver. He even had a sign with our names on it!

The next morning, we called a taxi to take us to Universal Studios. When the driver arrived, we told him where we wanted to go and he laughed—turns out Universal is only 200 feet away from our hotel.

We had a pretty cool moment at lunch. As we were eating, we noticed Mario Lopez sitting directly across from us! We ended up seeing him later at the filming of live TV show Extra.

The next day was finally Nickelodeon day! We were all *so* excited—we even had our own VIP passes! Our tour guide took us to where all the magic happens behind the scenes, where we saw the stars getting ready to perform.

Next, we got to watch Game Shakers live! The show was so funny and amazing. The best part? The kids on the show were just kids like me—they goofed around in between sets and got to work when it was time. We got to talk to them and take *tons* of pictures and then headed out.

I am grateful for this experience and would love to go back to LA!"

Carrie Siebert—Soap Commander
I signed up to receive the HARO emails, which arrive in my inbox 3 times a day, every weekday. My goal from the start has been to respond to at least 1 query every day (unless there isn't an applicable topic available) and to do so before that day's end. This has kept me consistent and motivated, especially in the beginning when I sent out responses for weeks without any feedback. And then, finally, there was a breakthrough! My first HARO pickup happened just this week and within the following 24 hours I was notified of TWO additional HARO wins. Wow!

As a small business owner, most of my pitches correspond to my entrepreneurial experience, but since I'm also a homeschooling mom, I always keep an eye out for queries involving family life. I was especially excited to get picked up for an article on mistakes to avoid when starting a family business. It was right up our alley!

Have a success story to share?
Please join the online conversation with hashtags:
#harosuccess
#poweroffreepublicity

Resources, References and Acknowledgements

Resources and References:
Help A Reporter Out—https://helpareporter.com
"Free Publicity: A TV Reporter Shares the Secrets for Getting Covered on the News" by Jeff Crilley, 2002
Joan Stewart—https://publicityhound.com
Business Insider—https://businessinsider.com
Source Bottle PR Service—http://www.sourcebottle.com

Acknowledgements:
Thank you so very much to everyone who contributed a story for the success section.

My Incredible First Editors:
Mac McCallum, Katy Tucker, Christine Laureano
The first team was amazing.

My next group of readers took me to the final stretch:
Jennifer Waller, Angela Bofill, Wendy Rubin, Michelle Tucker, Ross Perry, Holly Port, Amanda Aaron
Thank you for the great feedback and love.

Final Editor:
Loral Pepoon of Cowriterpro
Our meeting was fortuitous! Thank you for your encouragement and editing expertise.

About The Author

Roberta Perry

After years of being selfless and taking care of everyone else's needs, (OK, that is her humble opinion, but work with her here) Roberta's skin was dry, itchy and irritated. In 2005, at 43, she finally realized that taking care of her skin and herself was important. She discovered exfoliating products, but like the proverbial Goldilocks, none were completely satisfying her needs and wants. Roberta headed for the kitchen and played like a "mad chemist" to create her own. She mixed up different combinations of botanical oils, which she had read were great for skin. She did even more extensive research and realized how lucky she was with the recipe she had created. Roberta brought in her late sister and they started ScrubzBody™ Skin Care Products, in 2006, in her home. Marketing and getting exposure for the business on a tight budget was difficult, so Roberta turned to something better, free publicity. She has been using *Help a Reporter Out* since 2009 and believes it is the best of all the services that connect writers and reporters with the people who have stories to share.

She has been published and quoted in over 100+ skin care and business articles, blogs and beauty magazines. She was a panelist for the LI Newsday Connect Small Business Seminar, she was a guest for a natural remedy segment of the Dr. Oz show, which aired on 10/24/14, as well as a food related segment, which aired on 2/29/16. Roberta was a featured speaker on Indie Business Cruise 2016 about getting free publicity for your small business, which was the catalyst for this book. Roberta received the 2016 Nassau County Legislature Trailblazer award for her charity work.

In June of 2018, Roberta and the ScrubzBody team were featured as the finale episode on Season One of *Sell it Like Serhant*, on Bravo TV. Talk about Free Publicity!

Roberta is a proud member of Indie Business Network, American Made Matters, Farmingdale Chamber of Commerce and Bethpage Kiwanis Club.

ISBN 978-0-9978036-0-0